Success

Without Burnout

How to Win Big Without Losing Yourself

With PWT Mentor Experts

Annie Izmirliyan, Brian Crew, Carole Murko, Cheri Petroni, Dortha Hise, Dr. Carolina M. Billings, Dr. Norma Hollis, Dr. Patricia Suggs, Judy Cirullo, Lisa Li, Marlenne Doss, Mindy McManus, Monika Greczek, Sallie Wagner, Sara Notarfrancesco, Treva Graves, Wendy Vaughan, Youssef Skalli

Curated by
Dr. Carolina M. Billings
Founder
Powerful Women Today

Published by PWT Publishing
A division of Powerful Women Today
Greater Toronto Area, Ontario, Canada
Publisher: Dr. Carolina M. Billings' email: publisher@powerfulwomentoday.com

Design & Typesetting by: Dortha Hise
Cover Design by Dr. Carolina M. Billings

Limits of Liability and Disclaimer of Warranty
The author and publisher shall not be liable for the reader's misuse of this material. This book is strictly for informational and educational purposes.

Disclaimer
The views expressed are those of the author and do not reflect the official policy or position of the publisher or Powerful Women Today.

Copyright Use and Public Information
Unless otherwise noted, images have been used according to public information laws.

ISBN:
Paperback ISBN: 978-1-7382310-5-8
EBook ISBN: 978-1-7382310-8-9

Table of Contents

Preface

10 Truths about Women and Burnout

1. Women Are More Prone to Burnout Than Men

Research consistently shows that women experience higher levels of burnout than men. A McKinsey study found that *women are 1.5 times more likely to experience burnout* due to added pressures of balancing work, caregiving, and societal expectations. This imbalance is exacerbated by the *second shift* of domestic responsibilities.

2. The Invisible Labor Load

Many women carry the burden of *invisible labor,* which includes tasks like managing household schedules, emotional labor, and caregiving responsibilities. This mental load significantly increases stress levels, even when it isn't recognized or compensated.

3. Work-Life Balance Is Often Elusive

Despite the push for work-life balance, many women struggle to achieve it. Women are more likely to report feeling guilty about taking time for themselves, believing they need to *do it all,* which contributes to chronic stress and eventual burnout.

4. Cultural Expectations Amplify Pressure

Women often feel immense societal pressure to excel in multiple roles— professional, caregiver, partner, friend, and more. This expectation to *have it all* or *"be everything to everyone"* places an unrealistic and unsustainable burden on women, leading to exhaustion and burnout.

5. Burnout Impacts Women's Health Disproportionately

Burnout isn't just mental—it manifests physically. Women experiencing high levels of stress and burnout are more likely to suffer from heart disease, high blood pressure, sleep disorders, and autoimmune diseases. The chronic stress from burnout can also lead to more frequent illnesses due to a weakened immune system.

6. Women Often Internalize Stress

Instead of externalizing stress or seeking help, women are more likely to internalize their struggles, which leads to feelings of inadequacy, anxiety, and even depression. Society's norms about women being nurturers or caretakers often prevent them from expressing vulnerability or asking for support.

7. Burnout Is Especially Acute for Women of BIPOC heritage.

Bi-racial, Incigenous, People of Colour aka minority women within our North American experience, face even higher rates of burnout due to the added layers of racial and gender bias. They often feel the need to work harder to prove themselves in professional settings, leading to higher stress levels and less support or recognition for their work.

8. Perfectionism and Burnout Go Hand in Hand

Many women suffer from perfectionism, feeling they must perform flawlessly at work and in their personal lives. This constant striving for perfection is a significant contributor to burnout, as it leaves little room for rest, recovery, or self-compassion.

9. Leadership Roles Come with Increased Burnout Risk

Women in leadership roles are particularly vulnerable to burnout, especially if they are among the few women at the top. The pressure to succeed, be a role model, and break the glass ceiling often leaves women in these positions feeling isolated, overextended, and unsupported.

10. Self-Care Is Often Deprioritized

Women are often socialized to put others' needs before their own. As a result, self-care is viewed as selfish or indulgent. This *deprioritization* of their well-being accelerates burnout, as women feel they can't take time for themselves without neglecting other responsibilities.

These truths paint a complex picture of how societal roles, expectations, and internal pressures uniquely affect women's experiences with stress and burnout. Recognizing these challenges is the first step toward meaningful solutions that prioritize women's well-being and success.

10 Lies We Need to Stop Believing

Here are ten common lies we tell ourselves (and are told) about women, stress, and burnout, which often perpetuate harmful patterns and misconceptions:

1. Women Can Have It All Without Sacrifice

The myth that women can *have it all*—a thriving career, perfect family, social life, and personal well-being—without sacrifice sets an unrealistic standard. In reality, trying to do everything often leads to burnout and compromises in one or more areas of life.

2. Self-Care is Selfish

A persistent lie is that prioritizing self-care means neglecting your responsibilities to others. This makes women feel guilty for taking time for themselves, even though self-care is essential for long-term well-being and preventing burnout.

3. If You're Stressed, You're Not Managing Your Time Well

Stress is often framed as a personal failing, implying that if women were better at time management or more organized, they wouldn't be overwhelmed. In reality, stress often stems from unrealistic expectations, systemic pressures, and imbalanced workloads—not poor planning.

4. You Just Need to Try Harder

The idea that women can simply *push through* stress or burnout by working harder is dangerous. Burnout is not a sign of laziness or weakness, but a signal that the demands on a person have exceeded their resources, and more effort won't solve it.

5. Women Are Better at Multitasking

This myth reinforces the expectation that women should juggle multiple roles—career, family, home—seamlessly. Multitasking doesn't make women more efficient; it often leads to fragmented attention, increased stress, and ultimately, burnout.

6. Stress Means You're Doing Something Important

There's a belief that stress is a *badge of honour*, a sign that you're working hard and achieving great things. This lie glorifies stress and burnout, making it seem like a necessary part of success when in reality, chronic stress diminishes productivity, creativity, and happiness.

7. Burnout is Just a Personal Problem

Many think burnout is an individual issue, implying that it's up to each woman to *fix* herself. In truth, burnout is often the result of systemic issues—workplace cultures, societal expectations, and gender bias—that need to change.

8. Good Women Don't Complain

This harmful narrative suggests that women who speak out about their stress or burnout are whining or being weak. In reality, voicing these challenges is courageous and essential for creating healthier environments and addressing structural problems.

9. Taking Breaks Will Hurt Your Career

The fear that stepping back or taking a break will derail their careers prevents many women from prioritizing rest. In truth, regular breaks can improve productivity, creativity, and mental well-being, helping women sustain long-term success.

10. Successful Women Don't Get Burned Out

There's a false belief that if a woman is truly successful, she won't experience burnout, as if it's a sign of failure or inability to handle pressure. The reality is that burnout can happen to anyone, and recognizing it is the first step toward sustainable success.

These lies perpetuate unhealthy expectations and prevent women from addressing the root causes of stress and burnout. Acknowledging these myths is crucial to creating healthier narratives and practices that support women's well-being.

Call to Action to Kiss Burnout Goodbye

Are you ready to break free from the burnout cycle and reclaim your energy, your joy, and your success? It's time to stop believing the lies that have held you back and embrace the truth about what it really takes to thrive.

You don't have to sacrifice your well-being for your ambitions. *Success Without Burnout: How to Win Big Without Losing Yourself* is your guide to achieving your goals while preserving the most important thing—you.

Remember:

You are strong, resilient, and capable of more than you realize—but that doesn't mean you should have to choose between your health and your success.

You deserve a life where you can rise to the top without burning out along the way. By challenging the myths about stress and burnout, you can unlock a new path to sustainable success.

This book empowers you to win on your terms, giving you the tools to thrive in every area of life, without compromising who you are.

Let's do this,

Big Love

Carolina

www.Powerful Women Today.com

Introduction

Success Without Burnout: How to Win Big Without Losing Yourself

We've all seen it—the headlines that blare "Burnout Epidemic Hits Record Levels" or "Work Hard, Play Hard? No, Just Burnout Hard."

According to a recent study by Gallup, *76% of employees experience burnout at least some of the time* (Wigert & Agrawal, 2020). And it's not just about long hours—it's the emotional exhaustion, detachment, and feeling that you're stuck on a never-ending treadmill with no exit in sight. Sound familiar?

The world is obsessed with success, but the way we've been chasing it is leaving us depleted. We're told that winning requires sacrifice—our health, our happiness, our relationships—but that's an outdated mindset. Burnout is not a badge of honour. It's a crisis, and it's time for a new approach to success, one where you can achieve your biggest goals without losing yourself in the process.

What Problem Does This Book Solve?

The problem is simple yet widespread: burnout. We're burning out faster than ever before. The World Health Organization (WHO) has now classified burnout as an occupational phenomenon, and it's becoming increasingly clear that the way we pursue success needs a serious overhaul (WHO, 2019). Burnout not only impacts your productivity, but it also eats away at your mental and physical health, disrupts relationships, and diminishes the joy of achievement.

This book is here to change the narrative. Instead of pushing through exhaustion and thinking that success requires grinding yourself into the ground, we'll show you how to redefine success—on *your* terms. You'll learn strategies that don't just prevent burnout but empower you to thrive. Imagine accomplishing your biggest goals with energy, clarity, and the time to actually enjoy the fruits of your labor. That's what's in it for you.

Why Should We Care?

Because your life—your health, your happiness, and your purpose—are at stake. Burnout has real consequences. Research shows that individuals experiencing burnout are *63% more likely to take a sick day* and *23% more likely to visit the emergency room* (Keller, 2020). Let's be real: no amount of success is worth sacrificing your well-being. What's the point of winning if you're too exhausted to enjoy it?

"Your life—your health, your happiness, and your purpose—are at stake.

Burnout has real consequences"

Beyond personal stakes, burnout impacts your work, your leadership, and the teams or communities you serve. When you're running on empty, your creativity plummets, decision-making suffers, and your relationships become strained. The stakes are clear: success without balance leads to burnout, and burnout robs you of the very things you're working hard to achieve.

What is no longer working in the world today?

People today are trying to solve burnout through the typical "self-care" checklist—work-life balance tips, time management hacks, mindfulness apps, or weekend getaways. And while these solutions help momentarily, they don't address the root of the issue. You're still left juggling a million tasks, running on a timeline that's impossible to sustain, and feeling guilty if you're not constantly "on." Sure, you might feel refreshed for a moment after a yoga class or a digital detox, but by Monday morning, you're back in the grind, counting down the days to your next escape.

Leaders, too, are trying to tackle the burnout problem with wellness programs, shorter workweeks, or remote work flexibility, but these external solutions often miss the internal shift that's required. They're band-aids on a much deeper wound.

Speaking Truth to Power. Your Power.

Here's the tough truth: these solutions no longer work because they're surface-level fixes for a much deeper problem. The hustle culture that tells us to work harder, longer, and faster is deeply ingrained. While time management and mindfulness can help, they're not enough to combat the burnout epidemic if you're still buying into the idea that success requires sacrifice. The old formula of "grind now, rest later" is outdated, and quite frankly, it's broken.

The truth is, we need a new definition of success. One that includes space for rest, creativity, and joy—not just after you've "made it," but all along the way. We need to stop treating burnout like a rite of passage and start recognizing it as the red flag it is.

What Is to Be Gained by Opting Out?

What's to be gained from this shift is more than just energy—it's sustainable, meaningful success. When you learn to win without burning out, you gain a sense of fulfillment that goes beyond hitting financial or career milestones. You start building a life where success and happiness coexist, where your health and your goals are aligned, and where every win feels worth celebrating because you didn't sacrifice yourself to get there.

You will gain clarity on how to prioritize your energy, how to make decisions that serve both your ambitions and your well-being, and how to lead yourself and others in a way that doesn't just create short-term results, but long-term impact. In short, you'll gain *freedom*—freedom from the pressure to do it all, from the guilt of taking breaks, and from the exhaustion of constantly feeling behind.

Why we wrote this Guide for You

So, what's the solution? It's about adopting a mindset and strategy that puts *you* first. In this book, we'll guide you through actionable steps to redefine success in a way that sustains your energy, feeds your creativity, and honors your well-being. The ripple effect of this shift is huge. When you embrace this new definition of success, you'll not only thrive personally, but you'll also inspire those around you to do the same—your family, your colleagues, your team.

Imagine a world where success doesn't come at the cost of exhaustion but is built on a foundation of energy and joy. That's what we're here to help you create. Whether you're a high-powered executive, an entrepreneur, or someone climbing the ladder to your dreams, this book will give you the tools to get there without losing yourself along the way.

By shifting the way you think about success, you'll break free from the burnout cycle and unlock a new level of performance and fulfillment. As Arianna Huffington puts it, "Burnout is not the price you have to pay for success" (Huffington, 2016). And this book is here to show you exactly how to win *big*—without losing yourself in the process.

The Powerful Women Today Mentor Experts
We are #StrongerTogether

References

Huffington, A. (2016). *The Sleep Revolution: Transforming Your Life, One Night at a Time*. Harmony.

Keller, R. (2020). Burnout is wreaking havoc on workers and companies: Here's what needs to change. *Forbes*. Retrieved from https://www.forbes.com

Wigert, B., & Agrawal, S. (2020). Employee burnout: The biggest myth. *Gallup*. Retrieved from https://www.gallup.com

World Health Organization (WHO). (2019). Burn-out an "occupational phenomenon": International Classification of Diseases. Retrieved from https://www.who.int

"Doing the best at this moment puts you in the best place for the next moment."

Oprah Winfrey

Part 1: Mindset

Your mindset is the foundation of everything you do. It's the engine that drives your decisions, your reactions, and ultimately, your success.

Here's the thing—mindset isn't one-size-fits-all. The way you think, strategize, and approach challenges is as unique as you are. Some of you thrive on big-picture thinking, always ready to take bold steps toward your goals, while others excel in the details, ensuring nothing slips through the cracks. Maybe you're the person who brings passion and energy to every task, inspiring those around you. Or perhaps you're the steady, reliable force that keeps everything grounded and moving forward.

It's essential to know that your mindset can be the key to avoiding burnout while still achieving greatness. It's about recognizing your strengths, embracing how you operate, and adjusting when needed.

> **You're not here to fit into a mold—you're here to break it and create success on your terms, in a way that feels good and sustainable.**

In this section, we'll explore how to harness the power of your mindset to create a strategy that works for *you*. Because when you learn to work in alignment with your natural tendencies and enhance your mental resilience, you don't just win—you win without losing yourself in the process.

Let's dive in and discover how to make that mindset shift today!

"To all the empowered women who stand independent on solid ground."

HOW LIVING IN THE PRESENT WILL GUARANTEE YOUR FUTURE SUCCESS

by Dr. Carolina M. Billings

Chapter 1

How Living in the Present

Will Guarantee Your Future Success

By Dr. Carolina M. Billings

Let's start with a reality check: We are told to hustle, plan ahead, and have a five-year roadmap ready at all times living in a fast-paced, goal-driven world that's constantly pulling us in different directions. However,

" **Just because we are told something, does not mean we must agree or comply.**

Forget civil disobedience, this is a personal insurrection."

What if the key to your future success is not in obsessively planning for it, but in embracing where you are *right now*? Living in the present doesn't mean ignoring your future—it means making decisions today that will set the foundation for success, all while staying grounded and avoiding burnout.

The problem is simple, The Solution Even Simpler.

It is a matter of choice that is within your control. Yes, you have the power to choose. We are burning ourselves out by living too much in the future. Stress, anxiety, and pressure all come from trying to control things that haven't even happened yet. You feel that pull, don't you? The constant need to anticipate the next move, solve problems that may or may not arise, and hit goals that seem to stretch further with each passing day. Living in the present solves this by allowing you to stay focused on what you can control—*now*. It lets you make progress without getting lost in the *what-ifs*, creating a healthier and more effective path to success.

Here is the Shift that happens when living in the present.

The big win: peace of mind and laser focus right here, right now. By living in the moment, you free yourself from the mental drain of future worries. You'll make better decisions, increase productivity, and—most importantly—enjoy the journey. Imagine showing up fully to each task, conversation, and challenge with all your energy intact. When you do that, you're not only giving yourself the chance to perform at your best, but you're also setting the stage for your future success, one solid step at a time. You get to win big *and* stay refreshed, instead of running on fumes toward some far-off finish line.

Why This Is a Do or Die?

Why does this matter, you ask? I am glad you ask because your well-being, career, and relationships are at stake. Think about it: burnout happens when you're constantly pushing toward a future that feels out of reach. If you're always running, you're never truly *here*, and eventually, you'll hit a wall. Living in the present helps you avoid that wall altogether.

> *"Letting go of future expectations is the ultimate burnout prevention technique, keeping you grounded, engaged, and motivated— without the endless stress of chasing an ever-moving target."*

The cost of not living in the present is high. You risk your health, your mental clarity, and your joy. When you're constantly in future mode, it's easy to lose sight of what really matters: your well-being, your relationships, and the progress you're making in the here and now. If you don't make a shift, you might achieve success, but at what cost? You'll find yourself feeling exhausted, disconnected, and unfulfilled. The stakes are too high to ignore.

"If it cost you your peace, it is too expensive." - Paulo Coelho

Growing Burnout Crisis has Men Yelling and Women Exiting - Forbes

Recent data from the career resource site MyPerfectResume found that 88% of workers are burned out. It frequently leads to troublesome behaviour, creates a volatile workspace, and impacts their personal lives. Forbes May 2024.

A study published in the International Journal of Behavioral Medicine found that women were more likely to experience burnout than men, with rates of burnout among women being as much as 1.5 times higher than among men. LinkedIn.

Transforming FOMO into JOMO

The Joy of Missing Out: Right now, people are solving this problem by trying to balance it all—future planning, present obligations, and self-care. But let's be honest: the methods aren't working. You're likely bombarded with tips like "stay organized," "prioritize self-care," or "schedule time for mindfulness." And while those are great, they often add to the pressure instead of alleviating it. We're told to multitask our way through life, squeezing in meditation between meetings and hoping it's enough to keep us from collapsing at the end of the week.

Why the "balance everything" approach is outdated?

We're not machines, and the endless to-do list is never going to stop. Living for the future while juggling the present creates an internal tug-of-war, splitting your focus and draining your energy. The truth is this method doesn't just *not* work—it actively contributes to burnout. You're pulled in too many directions, leaving you feeling like you're constantly behind, even when you're moving forward.

When you shift to living fully in the present, you gain *control* over your time, energy, and outcomes. You stop worrying about tomorrow's challenges and focus on today's opportunities. This means better decisions, clearer thinking, and more genuine engagement with what's in front of you. The ripple effect is that you'll start to see the results you want without the overwhelming stress that typically accompanies high-level success. You gain clarity, confidence, and peace of mind—all while achieving your goals.

My Solution and Personal Practice: The Present-First Approach

So, how do you live in the present while still ensuring future success? It's all about adopting a *Present-First Approach*. This doesn't mean you ignore your goals; it means you prioritize the here and now because today's actions are what shape tomorrow's outcomes.

Here's how to make it work:

1. **Single Task, Single Focus:** Stop multitasking. Whatever is in front of you—whether it's a meeting, a project, or time with family—give it your full attention. When you focus fully on one thing, you're more effective, productive, and less stressed.
2. **Set Intentions, Not Just Goals:** Instead of obsessing over future outcomes, set daily intentions. What impact do you want to make today? How can you show up as your best self *right now*? This shifts your mindset from future anxiety to present empowerment.
3. **Practice Active Reflection:** At the end of each day, take a moment to reflect. What did you achieve today? What can you improve on tomorrow? This keeps you grounded in your progress without losing sight of your longer-term vision.
4. **Be Present in Conversations:** Whether you're leading a team or connecting with colleagues, practice deep listening and engagement. Don't let your mind wander to tomorrow's tasks. When you're present, you'll build stronger relationships, and people will feel your commitment and energy.
5. **Breathe and Reset:** Throughout your day, take mini-pauses to breathe and re-centre. It's a quick way to pull yourself back to the present moment when your mind starts racing ahead.

The Long-Term Effect: Success with Joy

When you embrace the Present-First Approach, the ripple effect is profound. You'll find that not only are you more successful, but you're also *happier* in the process. Your relationships will strengthen, your work will feel more meaningful, and you'll experience a deeper sense of satisfaction. Living in the present gives you the power to create a future you're proud of without sacrificing your well-being.

The best part? You'll discover that your future success is already taking shape, one present moment at a time. You won't have to chase it—it'll come to you as a natural result of your focus, presence, and authentic engagement with life. You'll win. not just in your career, but in your health, relationships, and overall sense of purpose.

This is your invitation to slow down, live fully, and succeed *without burnout,* you do not have anything to prove to anyone but yourself. It's not just possible— it's guaranteed when you embrace the power of the present. So, let's stop worrying about tomorrow and start thriving today!

Why I do what I do, with passion, without burnout.

**I live each second, of each minute, of each hour, of each day
Championing and Empowering Women's
Emotional and Financial Independence.
Because it is my oxygen and because**

Empowerment = Choices
Choices = Independence
Independence = Freedom

Do your *it* for *Yourself.*

About The Author

As the Founder and CEO of Powerful Women Today, a boutique incubator and accelerator agency for women's empowerment and brand optimization, I have been championing and enabling women's emotional and financial independence for over 13 years. With a vision and mission to help women achieve amazing goals and turn their vision into reality, I lead a global network of empowered women empowering each other through coaching, mentoring, training, publishing, broadcasting, and speaking.

I am also the Founder and CEO of The Hive Consulting Group, a strategic business growth and change leadership consultancy that leverages generative AI chatbots and marketing aggregates to support social and digital entrepreneurship for women. In my Doctoral research on the impact of these technologies on entrepreneurship, I have deep expertise and passion for innovation, transformation, and disruption.

My passion for Communications and Personal Branding has successfully championed numerous thought leaders. There is nothing I love more than helping go-getters get to their goals faster. My background in Marketing, Leadership, C-Suite, and Human Resources creates a fusion and innovative approach to help you with your visibility, impact and legacy goals.

Are you ready to level up and be a voice of positive change in the world?

CALL TO ACTION

Join our Global Network https://powerful-women-today.mn.co/?autojoin=1

Contact Info
Powerful Women Today
https://powerfulwomentoday.com/
carolina@powerfulwomentoday.com
https://www.linkedin.com/in/drcarolinambillings/

"Fearlessness is not the absence of fear. It's the mastery of fear."
Arianna Huffington

> "TO MY MENTORS WHO TAUGHT ME THE IMPORTANCE OF SELF CARE."

CREATING YOUR BEST SELF FOR YOUR BEST LIFE

by Monika Greczek

Chapter 2

Creating Your Best Self for Your Best Life

by Monika Greczek

Self-care goes beyond just pampering; it's a proactive way to nurture your overall well-being. By intentionally setting aside time for self-care, you are investing in your long-term mental and physical health. Regularly taking moments to unwind can prevent burnout, reduce stress levels, and even improve your immune system. In a world where we are constantly bombarded with responsibilities, deadlines, and distractions, having a personal space where you can disconnect, and recharge is invaluab e. An at-home spa allows you to do this on your own terms, providing an oasis of calm where you can focus on self-renewal, leaving you feeling more centred and refreshed.

Building Self-Care into Your Life

Self-care is all about ensuring that you take time to care for your physical, emotior al, and mental well-being. With our hectic lifestyles, it's easy to push self-care aside, but prioritizing it is crucial for your overall happiness and hea th. One of the simplest and most rewarding ways to practice self-care is by creating a personal spa experience at home. Not only is this option more affordable, but it also allows you to tailor the experience to your preferences. You can focus on the things that relax you most, from soothing music to your favourite essential oils and/cr skincare products. In this chapter, we will explore how an at-home spa can be beneficial for your health, your wallet, and your mood. Incorporating self-care rituals into your routine not only rejuvenates your body but also provides mental clarity, helping you stay balanced amid life's daily stresses.

With our hectic lifestyles, it's easy to push self-care aside, but prioritizing it is crucial for your overall happiness and health.

What is Self-Care?

Self-care refers to any intentional activity that promotes your well-being, whether it's physical, mental, or emotional. It's about maintaining balance and ensuring that you are healthy and happy, even when life's daily stresses build up. Recently, the importance of self-care has gained recognition, leading more people to integrate relaxing spa-like routines into their lives at home. These routines, whether they involve soaking in a warm bath, giving yourself a facial, or simply taking a moment to relax in a peaceful space, can work wonders for both your mind and body, helping to refresh and recharge you.

Why an At-Home Spa is Best

First, let's talk about the cost benefits. Professional spa treatments can be quite costly, with a single massage or facial often costing over $100. Regular visits can quickly add up, making it an expensive habit. In contrast, setting up your own spa at home allows you to invest in products like skincare items, a face mask, or essential oils that you can use repeatedly. This initial investment may seem like a lot, but in the long run, you'll save hundreds of dollars compared to frequenting a professional spa.

Moreover, an at-home spa offers unmatched convenience. You don't have to worry about making appointments, commuting, or planning around a spa's schedule. Whenever you have some spare time—whether it's after work, during a lazy weekend, or right before bed—you can enjoy your personal spa experience in the comfort of your own home. This flexibility makes it easier to prioritize self-care, ensuring it becomes a consistent part of your routine. In today's fast-paced world, the ability to pause and pamper yourself without the stress of travel or tight schedules is invaluable.

The beauty of an at-home spa is its *customizability*. You have the freedom to design an experience that truly relaxes and rejuvenates you. This could include calming music, fragrant essential oils, soft candlelight, or even a comfy robe. Whether you prefer a quiet, peaceful atmosphere or something more invigorating, the experience is entirely yours to craft. You can create an environment that meets your specific needs, allowing you to fully unwind and disconnect from stress, while also indulging in self-care practices that feel luxurious.

A Cleaner, Healthier Spa Experience

One significant advantage of having a spa at home is the ability to control the cleanliness of your environment. While professional spas do their best to maintain hygiene, you're sharing space and equipment with many other clients There's always a small risk of exposure to germs and bacteria. When you create a spa at home, you can ensure that your space and tools meet your personal standards of cleanliness, giving you peace of mind and reducing any worries about hygiene.

In addition, you have complete control over the products you use. If you have sensitive skin or specific preferences when it comes to ingredients, you can select hypoallergenic or organic products that work best for you. The ability to choose the perfect scents, like lavender or eucalyptus, and tailor the experience to your needs makes your spa session much more enjoyable and effective. Whether you prefer invigorating citrus aromas or calming floral fragrances, you can create the exact atmosphere that enhances your relaxation.

Benefits of regular *spa-like* self-care.

Regularly practicing self-care through spa-like routines is not a luxury—it's an essential part of maintaining your mental and emotional health. Taking even just 15 or 30 minutes for yourself sends an important message: that you are worth the time and care. This act of valuing yourself is key to mental well-being, reducing stress and improving emotional resilience. Creating a calming atmosphere at home with dim lghts, soft music, and soothing scents like lavender can help you establish a peaceful retreat in your everyday life.

> *"Taking even just 15 or 30 minutes for yourself sends an important message: that you are worth the time and care."*

Apart from the emotional benefits, spa rituals have physical benefits as well. A gentle massage can improve circulation, skin treatments can boost your complexion, and a warm bath can soothe tense muscles. Simple acts of self-care like exfoliating, hydrating, and moisturizing your skin regularly can lead to visible improvements over time. These little moments of care accumulate, leaving you feeling physically refreshed and more connected with your body. In the long run, a consistent spa habit can result in better overall health—both mental and physical.

Making It a Habit

To fully enjoy the benefits of an at-home spa routine, it's important to be consistent. Just like exercising or eating a balanced diet, self-care should be a regular part of your life. Start by setting aside a specific time in your weekly schedule, such as 30 minutes on Sunday evenings, to indulge in self-care activities.

You can also incorporate small rituals into your daily routine like a nighttime skincare routine to wind down before bed.

Creating a dedicated space for your spa activities can also help reinforce the habit. You don't need an entire room—just a cozy corner with your spa essentials like candles, essential oils, and soft blankets will do. Having a prepared space makes it easier to slip into relaxation mode, turning your spa routine into something you look forward to regularly. This designated area becomes a personal sanctuary, where you can disconnect from daily stress and focus on nurturing yourself.

Customer Experiences

Many people have found success and relaxation in creating their own at-home spa routines. Take Sarah, for instance. She's a busy mother of two, and for years, she used to visit professional spas for relaxation.

Now, instead of scheduling expensive treatments, she dedicates one evening each week to pampering herself at home with a foot bath, a collagen mask, and some quiet time. This new routine has not only saved her money but also helped her feel more relaxed and rejuvenated.

Similarly, Alex, a college student dealing with the stress of classes and exams, transformed a small corner of his dorm room into a personal spa. With essential oils, soft lighting, calming music, and an oversized bean bag. Alex created a space where he could unwind after long study sessions. This simple self-care practice helped him manage stress and stay focused on his studies.

Start Your Own Spa Routine Today

Regularly taking moments to unwind can prevent burnout, reduce stress levels, and even improve your immune system. In a world where we are constantly bombarded with responsibilities, deadlines, and distractions, having a personal space where you can disconnect, and recharge is invaluable. An at-home spa allows you to do this on your own terms, providing an oasis of calm where you can focus on self-renewal, leaving you feeling more centered and refreshed. Incorporating self-care rituals into your

routine not only rejuvenates your body but also provides mental clarity, helping you stay balanced amid life's daily stresses.

"Self-care extends beyond pampering; it's a proactive approach to nurturing your overall well-being. By intentionally dedicating time to self-care, you invest in your long-term mental and physical health."

An at-home spa routine offers a host of benefits, from saving money to giving you control over the products you use. The emotional and physical perks, such as stress relief and skin improvement, are undeniable. Now that you know how easy it is to set up your own personal spa, why not start your routine today? Taking care of yourself isn't a luxury—it's essential for staying healthy, both inside and out. With an at-home spa, you can enjoy the self-care you deserve whenever you need it, reminding yourself that you are worth it.

CALL TO ACTION

Learn more about The Virtual Spa: https://linktr.ee/extasyhairstudioandspa

About The Author:

For 36 years styling hair has been my passion because I enjoy the happiness that my customers achieve after they have their hair styled by me. During the 36 years I have learned to master the art of styling and love to use my creativity. I also learned the importance of taking care of our hair and body. I have attended massage therapy school and have been a massage therapist for 25 years. I have also attended makeup classes at MAC, Young Living and facial classes from Eminence, Farm House Fresh, and more. I also became a Yoga Instructor and Holistic Coach. Five years ago, I expanded my salon into a full-service salon and spa providing services such as organic facials, massages using essential oils, products that are para-bin, sulfate free, and better for us, using the most natural ingredients. My passion is to combine all the services to create a whole body, mind and soul experience for my clients at my world-renowned Holistic Salon and Spa.

Contact Info

The Virtua Spa

extasyhair@comcast.net

https://www.linkedin.com/company/101756614/admin/dashboard/

"To my soulmate, Jim.
I love you!"

BURNOUT: A PERSONAL JOURNEY AND THE PATH TO RECOVERY

by Carole Murko

Chapter 3

Burnout: A Personal Journey
and the Path to Recovery

By Carole Murko

As I sit down to write about burnout, I'll admit, I'm slightly burnt out. Isn't that ironic? The good news is that in just a few days, I'm heading to my heart home, Nantucket, Massachusetts, for a week of beach walks, sunsets, grilling, bonfires, and reunions with friends over fabulous dinners. The island embraced me during one of the hardest times of my life—a time when I was first diagnosed with a theoretically incurable eye disease.

When I reflect on what led to the onset of my illness, it's easy to trace it back to a lifetime spent in overdrive. I lived in a "programmed" reality of push, push, push; go, go, go; more, more, more. I truly believed I only needed 4 to 5 hours of sleep each night. By the time most people woke up, I had already lived 2 to 3 hours of my day. I was Superwoman—at least, that's what I told myself.

So many of us have been conditioned to keep that polished, shiny exterior intact while beneath it all, our bodies are crying out for help. For me, that cry started as migraines—an early warning signal that I was living out of alignment. Instead of stopping to evaluate the stressors or incorporate practices to manage them, I popped Excedrin, which led to a cascade of stomach issues and GERD.

On the outside, my life appeared perfect. I had an NPR radio show and had produced and hosted two nationally televised PBS specials. I was shiny, but on the inside, I was slowly tarnishing. I am here to tell you: don't be me. Don't ignore the signs your body gives you. Don't mask the symptoms with over-the-counter medications, hoping they'll just go away. Burnout is not something you "push through"—it's a recipe for disaster.

Before my diagnosis, everything in my life began to crumble. The Midas touch I once had vanished into thin air. My habitual drive—my constant pushing—was failing me. That's when a disease came out of nowhere as if to say, "Enough!" I found myself praying, wondering how I had reached this point. Then, as if by divine intervention, the universe sent me a sign: an opportunity on Nantucket. A friend called, offering me a job that was so below my skill level and pay grade, my first reaction was to say, "No way." But deep down, I knew that whatever I was doing at the time wasn't working. I was sick, nearly broke, and had nothing left to lose. So, I took the job.

What happened next was nothing short of miraculous.

Nantucket gave me a complete change of environment, a steady paycheck, and health insurance—something I desperately needed. But more than that, it gave me time. Time to reflect, to walk the beach each morning, and to turn inward. Those beach walks became my sanctuary, my church.

While I initially walked the Western medical path, I simultaneously opened myself to alternative modalities. I had always had a deep spiritual side, a connection to something greater than myself, but I didn't know how to access it fully. My diagnosis granted me permission to explore healing from within—to tune in to the idea that healing is an inside job.

The first radical change I made was to adopt an anti-inflammatory diet. I became obsessed with mastering how to make healing food not only nutritious but delicious. I also returned to a Qigong practice and became certified to teach it. Along my journey, I stumbled upon the teachings of Dr. Joe Dispenza. His work was so transformative for me that I eventually became certified to teach his methods as well.

Burnout is real. It creeps up on us, often subtly, manifesting as small, easily ignored symptoms. But left unchecked, it can lead to scary, life-altering diagnoses. The antidote to burnout begins in the mind. Our thoughts shape our reality. We are what we think, first. Then, we are what we eat.

As I prepare for my return to Nantucket, I feel a deep sense of gratitude for the lessons I've learned. Those beach walks taught me the importance of pausing, reflecting, and recharging. Now, I ensure that my life is filled with practices that keep me centered, grounded, and grateful.

Here is the recipe I follow to regulate my nervous system:

1. Journaling: Helps me connect with my thoughts. It's like having a personal therapist on call. Each day, I write down any thoughts that no longer serve me, like "I can't do this," and I replace them with empowering thoughts, such as "I can do this."

2. Mindfulness Practice: Conscious breathing and meditation are non-negotiable. Even if it's just five minutes of deep, intentional breathing, these practices create space for me to center myself.

3. Qigong: This moving meditation is my anchor. It opens up the body's energy pathways, bringing balance and flow to my system. I practice it daily, anc I teach it to others because it is so powerful. I call it a "wolf in sheep's clothing" because its simplicity belies its transformative power.

4. Gratitude Practice: Every morning, the first thing I write in my journal is, "Thank God I am alive in this body." Gratitude shifts my mindset and sets the tone for my day. At night, I jot down a quick gratitude list, reflecting on the blessings of the day.

5. Emotional Freedom Technique (EFT): When I feel stuck or blocked, I use EFT to tap into my body's energy meridians and release limiting beliefs. This practice helps me address specific issues like feelings of lack or unworthiness.

6. Intention Setting: Each day, I meditate with a clear intention for what I want to create. I enter my day with that focus, and if life throws me off balance, I pause, ground myself, and recalibrate through breathwork or Qi-marching.

It's easy to fall into the trap of believing that busyness equals success, that pushing through the exhaustion is a badge of honor. But, as I've learned the hard way, that mindset will eventually lead to burnout.

My practices are now as essential to me as brushing my teeth or taking a shower. They are the foundation of my health, happiness, and well-being. Burnout isn't inevitable. With the right mindset and tools, we can prevent it. But 't requires

vigilance, awareness, and most importantly, self-love.

So, find your Nantucket, wherever that may be. Create rituals that nourish

your mind, body, and soul. And above all, remember to be grateful for yourself—

for your strength, resilience, and capacity to heal.

Here are some additional steps to protect yourself from burnout:

- Stop Complaining: Whether it's about the weather or the traffic, complaints drain

your energy.

- Release Judgment: Judging yourself or others is an unconscious habit that breeds

negativity.

- Turn Off the News: Constant exposure to negativity fuels stress. Choose what you

allow into your mind.

Final Thoughts:

Burnout isn't something that just happens to us. It's the result of cumulative

stress, ignored signs, and a disconnect from our true selves. By becoming familiar

with your thoughts, recognizing the link between your thoughts and feel ngs, and

implementing practices to shift those patterns, you can live a life free from burnout.

Be intentional, be present, and always, always practice gratitude.

CALL TO ACTION

Book a Free Coaching Call with Carole: https://calendly.com/carolem/30-minute-coaching

About The Author

Carole Murko is a Mindset, Self-Mastery, and Health Coach dedicated to helping individuals activate the healer within. She is the founder of **Love.Eat.Heal**, a wellness platform that promotes self-love, conscious eating, and practices like breathwork, meditation, and journaling. With a multifaceted career path, Carole has seamlessly transitioned from analyzing municipal bonds at Moody's and leading global marketing at State Street Global Advisors to decorating celebrity homes and producing and hosting NPR and PBS shows, including *Heirloom Meals*.

A rare, incurable eye disease diagnosis led Carole on a profound healing journey. Embracing meditation, nutrition, and consciousness, she transformed her life and became passionate about guiding others through their own healing processes. As a NeuroChange Solutions Consultant, Carole now teaches Dr. Joe Dispenza's "Change Your Mind, Create New Results" program, helping corporate leaders, entrepreneurs, and individuals facing chronic illness to create lasting, conscious change.

Carole's mission is to empower people to reconnect with themselves, shift their mindsets, and use the power of the mind-body connection to achieve optimal health and well-being. With certifications in herbalism, health coaching, cannabis coaching, and Dragon's Way Qigong instruction, Carole blends science, spirituality, and personal experience to offer a holistic approach to self-mastery.

When she's not coaching, Carole enjoys cooking, gardening, needlepointing, and spending time with her husband and their beloved border collies.

Carole Murko | Love. Eat. Heal.

www.loveeatheal.com

carole@loveeatheal.com

https://www.linkedin.com/in/carole-murko-2b310b/

"To all the mentors who believed in me, guided me, and lit the path to my confidence—this chapter is for you."

CONFIDENT AND UNSTOPPABLE: THE SECRET TO SUCCESS WITHOUT BURNING OUT.

by Treva Graves

Chapter 4

Confident and Unstoppable:

The Secret to Success Without Burning Out

Treva Graves

The concept of success is often linked to long hours, constant hustle, and a relentless drive for more. However, this approach often leads to burnout, leaving individuals drained and disconnected from their true selves. In contrast, confidence plays a pivotal role in achieving meaningful success without sacrificing well-being.

Confidence is not just about feeling good about yourself; it's a powerful tool that guides how you manage your energy, set boundaries, and stay aligned with your values. This balance is essential to winning big without losing yourself in the process. In this exploration of confidence and sustainable success, we'll delve into five key areas where confidence enables you to achieve your goals without burning out: trusting your priorities, setting boundaries, managing perfectionism, cultivating resilience, and sustaining motivation.

Trusting Your Priorities: Confidence in Your Path

One of the first areas where confidence is essential is in trusting your priorities. In a world full of distractions and competing demands, it's easy to lose sight of what truly matters. Confident individuals have clarity about their values and goals, which enables them to prioritize tasks and commitments that align with their purpose. When you're confident in your priorities, you're less likely to be swayed by external pressures or to get caught up in activities that don't serve your long-term vision.

For instance, consider someone who is building a business while balancing family responsibilities. Without confidence, they might feel obligated to say yes to every opportunity, attend every networking event, and take on every client—even if it leads to overwork and stress. On the other hand, someone who trusts their priorities will make decisions based on what's most aligned with their goals, whether that's focusing on a key project, spending quality time with family, or investing in self-care. This clarity and confidence prevent them from overcommitting and helps them focus on high-impact activities that lead to sustainable success.

Setting Boundaries: Protecting Your Time and Energy

Setting and maintaining boundaries is one of the most powerful ways to avoid burnout, and confidence is essential in doing this effectively. People often struggle with saying no because they fear disappointing others or missing out on opportunities. However, confidence allows you to assert your needs without guilt or fear. When you're confident in your worth and value, you understand that protecting your time and energy is crucial to long-term success.

Boundaries can take many forms. They might involve limiting work hours, declining requests that don't align with your goals, or creating space for rest and rejuvenation. For example, a confident professional might decide that after 6 p.m., they won't respond to work emails or take business calls. This boundary ensures that they have time to recharge and maintain their well-being, which ultimately enhances their performance when they're working. Similarly, confident individuals might be selective about the projects they take on, focusing only on those that are in line with their expertise and passion. By saying no to the wrong things, they create more room for the right opportunities—those that align with their values and support their growth.

In addition to external boundaries, confidence also helps with setting internal boundaries. This involves managing self-expectations and resisting the urge to push yourself too hard. Confident individuals recognize when it's time to take a break and understand that rest is not a sign of weakness, but a necessary part of sustainable success.

> *"Setting and maintaining boundaries*
> *is one of the most powerful ways to avoid burnout, and confidence is*
> *essential in doing this effectively."*

Managing Perfectionism: Embracing Progress Over Perfection

Perfectionism is a major driver of burnout, especially among high achievers. The constant striving for flawlessness can lead to overwork, self-criticism, and dissatisfaction—even when things are going well. Confidence is a key factor in overcoming perfectionism because it allows you to embrace progress over perfection. When you're confident in your abilities and worth, you're more likely to accept that doing your best is enough, even if it's not perfect.

Confident individuals understand that perfection is an illusion and that waiting until something is flawless often leads to missed opportunities and unnecessary stress. Instead of getting caught up in the details, they focus on taking consistent action and learning from the process. This approach not only reduces the pressure but also leads to faster growth and better outcomes. For example, someone working on a major project might set a goal of completing a task to the best of their ability within a set timeframe, rather than endlessly refining it. This mindset shift from perfection to progress helps them maintain momentum without exhausting themselves.

Moreover, confidence helps you separate your self-worth from your achievements. Perfectionists often tie their sense of value to external validation, which makes them more vulnerable to burnout when things don't go as planned. Confident individuals, on the other hand, recognize that their worth isn't dependent on being perfect. This inner assurance allows them to be more forgiving of themselves, to learn from mistakes without spiraling into self-doubt, and to stay focused on their long-term vision.

Cultivating Resilience: Bouncing Back from Setbacks

Resilience is the ability to recover from setbacks and keep moving forward, and it's closely tied to confidence. No matter how skilled or experienced you are, challenges and failures are inevitable on the path to success. What sets confident individuals apart is how they respond to these obstacles. Instead of seeing setbacks as a reflection of their abilities, they view them as opportunities for growth and learning.

Confidence gives you the perspective needed to bounce back from failures without internalizing them. When faced with a challenge, confident individuals don't dwell on what went wrong; instead, they focus on finding solutions and adapting their approach. This resilience is crucial in avoiding burnout because it prevents you from getting stuck in negative thought patterns that drain your energy and motivation.

"Confidence gives you the perspective needed to bounce back from failures without internalizing them."

For example, imagine a business owner who experiences a significant financial loss due to a failed product launch. Someone lacking confidence might see this as proof that they're not cut out for entrepreneurship and consider giving up. A confident individual, however, would analyze what went wrong, learn from the experience, and use that knowledge to improve future efforts. This ability to stay resilient in the face of adversity not only keeps you on track toward your goals but also protects your mental and emotional well-being.

Additionally, confidence helps you build a support system that further bolsters resilience. When you're confident, you're more likely to seek out mentors, peers, and resources that can help you navigate challenges. Rather than feeling isolated or afraid to ask for help, you recognize that collaboration and community are essential for sustainable success. This network of support can make all the difference in preventing burnout during tough times.

Sustaining Motivation: Believing in Your Ability to Succeed

Confidence is the driving force behind sustained motivation. It's easy to stay motivated when things are going well, but true success requires the ability to stay committed even when the journey is difficult. Confidence gives you the belief that you're capable of achieving your goals, no matter how ambitious they are. This self-assurance fuels your determination and keeps you focused on the bigger picture, even when progress seems slow.

When you believe in your ability to succeed, you're more likely to take consistent action toward your goals. This consistency is key to achieving long-term success without burning out. Rather than pushing yourself to the brink in short bursts of intense effort, confident individuals pace themselves, understanding that slow and steady progress leads to more sustainable results. They trust that their efforts will pay off over time, which helps them stay patient and avoid the all-or-nothing mentality that often leads to burnout.

Confidence also helps you stay motivated by keeping you connected to your "why." When you're clear about why you're pursuing a goal—whether it's for personal fulfillment, financial freedom, or making a positive impact—you're more likely to stay engaged and inspired, even when challenges arise. This sense of purpose is a powerful antidote to burnout because it reminds you that your work is meaningful, which keeps you going when the road gets tough.

Finally, confidence encourages you to celebrate small wins along the way. High achievers often overlook their progress in pursuit of bigger milestones, but confident individuals understand the importance of recognizing and appreciating every step forward. These celebrations not only boost motivation but also reinforce the belief that you're on the right track, which helps you stay energized and focused.

The Confidence to Win Big Without Losing Yourself

Confidence is more than just a feeling; it's a strategic asset that allows you to achieve success on your terms. By trusting your priorities, setting boundaries, managing perfectionism, cultivating resilience, and sustaining motivation, confidence empowers you to pursue ambitious goals without compromising your well-being. This balanced approach to success is what makes it possible to win big without losing yourself in the process.

Our world often glorifies overwork and hustle, it's important to remember that true success isn't about how much you can do—it's about how effectively you can achieve your goals while staying true to who you are. Confidence is the foundation that enables you to navigate this path with clarity, purpose, and grace. It allows you to define success on your terms, set boundaries that protect your energy, and stay resilient in the face of challenges. With confidence, you can achieve remarkable results while maintaining the balance, fulfillment, and well-being needed to enjoy the journey.

CALL TO ACTION

Ready to break free from the grip of perfectionism? It's time to embrace progress over perfection and take back control of your life. Start by letting go of unrealistic expectations that create burnout and celebrate each step forward. You deserve to live with confidence, not constant pressure.

Take the first step today and commit to progress, not perfection, by downloading my free Progress over Perfection Challenge.

https://mailchi.mp/bloompersonalbranding/the-perfection-over-progress-challenge

About The Author

As the CEO & Founder of Bloom Personal Branding, Treva Graves is an empowering coach, dynamic speaker and author delivering impactful presentations on topics including using neuroscience to master confidence, personal branding, and rethinking imposter syndrome. Her engaging and relatable style resonates with women at all stages of their careers, from emerging leaders to established executives. Through her talks, she offers actionable strategies that help women gain clarity, build resilience, and take charge of their personal and professional lives.

In addition to her speaking engagements, Treva offers Flourish Women's Retreat, 1:1 coaching, group workshops, a membership community and online courses that provide practical tools and insights for women looking to transform their mindset and elevate their confidence. Her programs are designed to address unique challenges high-achieving women face, helping them overcome perfectionism, silence their inner critic, and develop a strong personal brand that reflects their true potential. As a trusted coach, role model and mentor, Treva brings a holistic approach to confidence building, guiding women to align their internal beliefs with their external presence.

A skilled expert in her field, Treva is a mentor expert at Powerful Women Today and best-selling author of Self-Doubt Detox. She is an executive contributor for Brainz Magazine and is the recipient of the 2024 CREA Global Award in recognition of her leadership, creative and innovative ideas, and adaptability in business. She has over 12 professional certifications and holds bachelor's and master's degrees in business management and communication science from the University of South Dakota.

Contact Info

Bloom Personal Branding

https://www.bloompersonalbranding.com

treva@bloompersonalbranding.com

https://www.linkedin.com/in/trevagraves

"You cannot talk about success without talking about failure. Failure is part of the process."

Brené Brown

"To my husband, Paul, and my children, Malakai and Noah, as well as to all my fellow entrepreneurs who are not afraid to go against the grain."

LIVING MY PERFECTLY UNBALANCED LIFE

by Marlenne Doss

Chapter 5

Living My Perfectly Unbalanced Life

by Marlenne Doss, B.Sc.(Hons.), LL.B.

f you talk to a hundred people, they would each probably have their own definition of success. When thinking about myself and what I would define as success, there are a few prongs I would explore – my family, my personal relationships, my spirituality, my finances and my business. Each area comes with its challenges and with the constant struggle of wanting to strive for more without losing oneself. I know I have faced this regularly and still find it challenging sometimes to find a sense of balance.

Before getting into that, I should tell you a bit about me. I just celebrated my ten-year anniversary with my husband, Paul. We have two young boys. I work as a lawyer and have been running my own business for about 15 years now. I am also involved in other ventures not related to my law practice, focused on one of my greatest passions, empowering and uplifting youth. Almost everything I do is motivated by my desire to create a legacy for my family. My family also forces me to keep a constant check and balance of myself, including my time management, stress management and priorities.

For me, and I suspect that some of you can relate to this, wearing so many hats means that I do not define success the same way others might. I do not believe in 'balance' the way some people might speak of it. But I do believe that success means being able to do what you love with and for the people you love as frequently as you want to and being able to live your life's purpose.

I cannot say that I have fully mastered this or reached my ultimate goals, but I am constantly moving in the right direction. To me, success is a journey, rather than a destination, comprised of a series of milestones. Each one brings with it its own tests and lessons.

> **"I suspect that some of you can relate to this, wearing so many hats means that I do not define success the same way others might"**

I also fully acknowledge that there are often competing interests when striving towards a goal and sacrifices are constantly required. This struggle for me in the past has certainly led to feelings of burnout at times. It is impossible to show up 100% of the time in full throttle. I would feel like I was being pulled by my arms and legs in four different directions.

So, I have concluded that there is no real balance for me, not in the way I have heard others speak about it. Of the five prongs I mentioned earlier, each one does not get 20% of my time and energy each day and my day does not consist of a 9-5 schedule, followed by evenings of idleness. And I love that! Once I made my peace with my reality, I was able to let go of the stress of finding 'balance' and the guilt and stress of constantly falling short of the unreasonable expectations I had placed on myself. This definitely reduced my trips towards burnout.

> **"I have concluded that there is no real balance for me,**
>
> **not in the way I have heard others speak about it."**

I also realized that the more time I spent doing what I love, whether in my personal or professional life, the more energy I had and enjoyment I took in what I was doing. I was able to be present in the way I wanted to be and in the way that the people, clients and loved ones around me deserved. This certainly meant that my circle of friends shrank over time and the things that I said 'yes' to were well thought-out before I committed to them.

The other priority for me that has helped me stay on track is focusing on my spiritual growth and health. This has been my saving grace. I am a Christian by faith and my faith has helped me grapple with moments that would have otherwise left me spiraling because of feelings of a loss of control or questions of 'why'. Things happen that I do not want to happen and that can sometimes bring me to my knees.

But what enables me to get up again is hope for my future and a belief that these

things are happening *for* me rather than *to* me.

> *"The other priority for me that has helped me stay on track*
>
> *is focusing on my spiritual growth and health."*

I have been told that a rocket fails on its way to its destination. It sets a target

and readjusts all the way to it. I believe we are built similarly. We are goal-seeking

organisms that must fail and recalibrate all the way to our goals, especially the big

important ones. On the way, we inevitably reach roadblocks, fears, things out of

our control, unexpected things. But it is only when we retreat or quit that we

actually fail. Otherwise, as I heard it said, my tests can be (and have been) my

testimony.

Throughout my life and career, I have faced these types of moments, but

now my faith and my shift in mindset help me ride the waves. I can focus better on

finding the solutions or at least the lessons in the losses or challenges. Every lesson

I have learned has not come from smooth sailing moments but from the moments

that have forced me to be stretched and taken out of my comfort zone. This usually

meant I needed to ask for help from someone, which I learned to do quite readily.

I have no problem seeking help from others who are more knowledgeable or skilled in relationships, mindset, finances and business than me. It is so unnecessary to try to learn everything on our own.

Also, it has been a great gift to learn to delegate things. For instance, I used to feel so guilty that my house was not being kept clean the way I wanted for my children, but for many reasons, I resisted the idea of hiring someone to take care of this for me. I finally did and years later I have absolutely no regrets. It freed up time and mental space knowing the issue was being addressed. Delegation is the only way to regain time and grow your business, I believe.

Another key lesson has been to stop comparing myself to anyone else. Inevitably someone will look like they are way ahead of you, or their journey may appear like it was easier. But it is different for each one of us with our experiences, gestation periods, and the time it takes us to learn the lessons needed to become who we need to be to elevate to our next step.

It was a waste of energy to compare myself to anyone else. More importantly, it was very toxic. It was such a negative unproductive, scarcity-focused mindset. Shifting the focus to me – what I was doing right, what needed to be worked on, what goals I needed to set, and who I needed to connect with – were all better uses of my energy and kept me moving forward and expanding. I learned to also always find gratitude, regardless of my circumstances. There was always something good that if I took the time to appreciate, would help me snap out of any negative emotions I was experiencing and remind me that the setbacks were momentary and would not determine my future.

"It was a waste of energy to compare myself to anyone else. More importantly, it was very toxic. It was such a negative unproductive, scarcity-focused mindset."

The more focused I remain on hope, and on my goals and opportunities, the less exhausted I am, and the more opportunities come my way. This literally reduces my chances of burning out and getting depressed, consequently keeping me healthy.

I plan to keep setting higher and more unreasonable goals and when I reach them, to set even higher ones. After all, as I said, it is all about the journey. I have not heard one person say that their greatest lessons came from reaching their pinnacles. The lessons always come from the climb up.

In that regard, I learned to always invest in myself. I strive to increase in knowledge and expertise continuously, to surround myself with like-minded individuals, to prioritize my time off (for my family as much as for me), to learn about investments, focus on creating a retirement plan and on creating a legacy plan that s best for my family.

Setting up a retirement plan, which includes purchasing the appropriate life insurance policies and creating an investment plan, is very empowering. While the plan is still underway and I am not quite ready to retire, it still gives me a sense of control and comfort. In addition, setting up my husband and my estate plans gave me such peace of mind. Having the challenging conversations and making decisions regarding our children in the event neither of us is around and then putting that plan in place with our wills and powers of attorney gave us such peace of mind and was the responsible thing to do.

This is why I love my profession. In a small way, I can make sure that people like you and I can take a little more control of our lives and offer our loved ones the protection they need and deserve. In my experience, the most anxiety-provoking things are the things I feel I have the least control over. Knowing that I am doing everything in my power to set myself and my family up for success gives me great comfort. a comfort that I want all of you to experience as well. If I can be of assistance in any way on your journeys, just reach out.

CALL TO ACTION Get in touch with me right away to put your family's estate plans in place now.

About The Author

Marlenne has been practicing law since 2005. She obtained her law degree from Queen's University. Prior to this, she graduated from the University of Toronto with an Honors Bachelor of Science degree in Neuroscience and Psychology.

Marlenne is a founding partner at Aion Law Partners, priding herself on providing the service and experience of a large firm without losing the personal touch, client care and compassion of a small firm. Her practice is focused on estate planning, estate administration, real estate law and corporate law. She feels these areas of law impact people and their families the most, so she makes a real difference with the legal services she provides.

Marlenne prides herself on providing her clients with expert service, while ensuring utmost compassion and integrity are maintained in all her dealings. She is passionate about educating her clients so that together they can take a preventive and personalized approach to help them reach the goals they want for themselves and their families.

Marlenne is also actively involved in providing seminars on various legal topics to the community and to various businesses. She is madly in love with her two young boys and supportive husband. In her down time, she enjoys time with her family and close friends, travelling, and cooking.

If you would like to contact her, you can reach her at 866-246-6529 or marlenne@aionlaw.ca. You can also read more about her at https://www.aionlaw.ca, follow her on LinkedIn and Instagram.

Contact Info

Aion Law Partners LLP

www.aionlaw.ca

marlenne@aionlaw.ca

https://www.linkedin.com/in/marlenne-doss-90564120/

"To my husband."

HOW DELEGATION AND NATURE HELPED ME AVOID BURNOUT

by Dortha Hise

Chapter 6

How Delegation and Nature
Helped Me Avoid Burnout

By Dortha Hise

Reality check: being an entrepreneur can feel like a never-ending marathon at a sprint pace.

You are juggling a million things at once, doing everything to keep your business thriving while also managing the demands of everyday life. It is easy to slip into the mindset that "you have to do it all yourself," right? Unfortunately, that often leads to burnout. As an entrepreneur, I've always been driven to achieve. My journey to understanding the true power of delegation and the healing effects of nature came through unexpected and challenging experiences. I am going to share a bit of what I learned in my journey to avoid burnout and hope it helps others do the same.

The Weight of Overwhelm

My wake-up call did not come in a boardroom or during a client meeting. It came in waves of loss and personal challenges that would have knocked many people down for good. In just two years, I experienced the deaths of 28 people close to me. The weight of grief was immense, and, life wasn't done testing my resilience.

As if the emotional toll wasn't enough, I also lost my voice during that time. At first, I thought it was just laryngitis or bronchitis - something that would pass. Yet, the diagnosis was far more complex: Abductor Spasmodic Dysphonia (AB SD), a neurological condition that prevented me from using the phone, speaking normally, or being easily heard in noisy environments.

For someone whose business relied heavily on communication, this felt like a potential career-ender. How could I lead, coach, or give presentations if I couldn't speak effectively?

Burnout isn't just feeling tired; it's a state of physical, emotional, and mental exhaustion that can have serious consequences.

Here are some ways burnout might show up:

1. **Physical symptoms:** Constant fatigue, headaches, muscle tension, or even more serious health issues like high blood pressure or a weakened immune system.

2. **Emotional changes**: Irritability, anxiety, depression, or a sense of detachment from your work and personal life.

3. **Mental fog:** Difficulty concentrating, making decisions, or coming up with creative solutions – the very skills that are crucial for your business success.

4. **Strained relationships**: When work consumes all your time and energy, connections with family and friends inevitably suffer. You might find yourself missing important events or being physically present but mentally absent.

5. **Loss of passion:** The excitement and drive that once fueled your entrepreneurial journey can be extinguished by chronic overwork, leaving you questioning why you started this journey in the first place.

The irony is that in our attempt to do everything, we often end up achieving less. Our productivity suffers, our decision-making becomes impaired, and we lose sight of the big picture that's so crucial for business growth.

Discovering Hidden Strengths

This was when I began to truly understand the power of delegation. Out of necessity I had to find new ways to communicate and run my business. I learned to lean on my team more, to trust others with tasks I previously thought only I could handle.

Something unexpected happened as I adapted to my new reality. My condition, which I initially saw as a weakness, became a strength. It heightened my ability to listen deeply, to pick up on nuances in communication that I might have missed before. This newfound skill proved invaluable in understanding and addressing the needs of my high-achieving clients.

The Hea ing Power of Nature

While I was making strides in my professional life, I still felt overwhelmed. That's when nature stepped in to teach me its most profound lesson.

In 2015, my husband and I were invited to join a three-day backpacking trip with a colleague of his from work. At the beginning of that trip, I set an intention "to be open to whatever I was meant to receive on the journey." Little did I know *how transformative* it would be.

Surrounded by the quiet majesty of the Sierra Nevada mountains, away from the constant demands of technology and business, I found a clarity I hadn't experienced in years. The physical exertion of hiking, the fresh air, the sheer beauty of my surroundings - all combined to give me a perspective that was impossible to achieve from behind my desk.

When I returned home, I realized that this experience had expanded my resilience in ways I never expected. The final act of letting go - of expectations, of the need to control everything - brought the ultimate antidote to overwhelm.

The Transformation

Integrating time in nature into my routine became non-negotiable. I blocked off time in my calendar for our outdoor adventures just as I would for any important business appointment. The effects were and continue to be profound. I returned from these adventures feeling energized and clear-headed. Problems that had seemed insurmountable often resolved themselves after a long walk in the woods.

More importantly, I was happier – like in my soul. The joy I had felt at the beginning of my entrepreneurial journey returned. I was present in my personal life without the constant pull of work-related stress.

A Different Way Forward

Today, my approach to work and life is radically different from where I started. Delegation is no longer a last resort but a core part of my business strategy. I've built a team I trust, and I'm continually looking for ways to empower them to take on more responsibility.

As for nature, it's become my not-so-secret weapon for maintaining balance and perspective. Whether it's a multi-day backpacking trip or a quick hike before or after work, I prioritize my time outdoors. It's non-negotiable self-care that makes me a better entrepreneur, leader, and person.

Sharing the Journey

My experience taught me that burnout is not an inevitable part of entrepreneurship or high achievement. It's possible to build a successful business without sacrificing your health, relationships, or passions. That's why I became a certified coach, teaching others the techniques I developed both strategically and intuitively.

If my story resonates with you—if you're feeling overwhelmed and ready for a change—here are some actionable steps you can take to find your own path to balance:

1. **Identify your overwhelm**: Take a moment to jot down everything that's currently weighing on you. What tasks do you dread? What responsibilities feel too heavy? This exercise will help you clarify what needs to change.

2. **Start delegating**: Choose one or two tasks from your list that you can delegate. This could be anything from managing your social media accounts to handling customer inquiries. If you don't have a team yet, consider hiring a virtual assistant or asking a friend for help.

3. **Create clear processes**: For the tasks you're delegating, outline clear steps and expectations. Write down instructions or create simple guides that make it easy for someone else to take over. This will help ensure that the work is done to your standards without needing constant oversight.

4. **Schedule regular breaks**: Make self-care a priority by scheduling breaks throughout your day. Set alarms on your phone as reminders to step away from your desk, stretch, or take a few deep breaths. These small pauses can significantly boost your productivity and mental clarity.

5. **Reconnect with nature**: Plan a hike or outdoor activity this week. Whether it's a short walk in your neighbourhood park or a weekend backpacking trip, getting outside can help clear your mind and recharge your spirit. Consider

setting a regular outdoor date with yourself—maybe once a week—to ensure you make it a habit.

6. **Set boundaries**: Establish clear work hours and stick to them. Communicate these boundaries with your team and clients so they know when you're available. Protecting your personal time is crucial for maintaining balance.

7. **Reflect on your progress**: At the end of each week, take some time to reflect on what worked and what didn't in terms of delegation and self-care. Adjust your strategies as needed and celebrate any small wins along the way.

8. **Get support**: If you're feeling stuck or unsure where to start, consider reaching out for support. Whether it's joining a coaching program, finding an accountability partner, or simply talking with friends about your challenges, having support can make all the difference.

9. **Other occurrences:** at a personal level, we see the tug-of-war between delegation, control, and trust in all areas of our lives. Once we become aware of it in one area, it becomes known in other areas, too.

"You do not have to navigate this journey alone. Together, we can create a strategy that allows you to thrive both personally and professionally."

CALL TO ACTION

If you are ready to reclaim your time, rediscover and reconnect to your passion, and build a business that energizes rather than drains you, I invite you to connect with me on social media. And be sure to grab my free Breath Self-Compassion Guided Meditation to give yourself the gift of self-care right now: https://morning-sunset-80786.myflodesk.com/breathing-self-compassion

About The Author

Dortha Hise is an international bestselling author and the founder of Summit to Your Success, where she serves as the Chief Overwhelm Solver and Productivity & Delegation Optimizer. With a unique blend of business acumen and personal resilience, Dortha specializes in helping high-achieving professionals reclaim their time through strategic automation and delegation techniques.

Dortha's journey to becoming a productivity expert was shaped by profound personal challenges, including a neurological condition that temporarily silenced her voice. This experience deepened her ability to listen and reinforced her resilience, skills she now leverages to help clients navigate their own obstacles.

A certified coach and nature enthusiast, Dortha discovered the transformative power of "disconnecting to reconnect" during a pivotal backpacking trip in 2015. This experience inspired her to integrate mindfulness and intention-setting into her coaching methodology, helping clients find balance amidst the demands of high-performance careers and businesses.

Dortha's work has been featured in international bestselling books, and she is a sought-after speaker on topics related to productivity, delegation, and overcoming overwhelm. Through her writing, coaching, and speaking engagements, Dortha continues to inspire individuals to optimize their performance without sacrificing their well-being.

Contact Info

Summit to Your Success

https://summittoyoursuccess.com/

dortha@summittoyoursuccess.com

https://www.linkedin.com/in/dorthahise/

"To my husband, Jimi."

STRESS-FREE SUCCESS: FINDING BALANCE THROUGH FAITH

by Mindy McManus

Chapter 7

Stress-Free Success: Finding Balance Through Faith

by Mindy McManus

The Price of Stress

Stress often becomes an unwelcome but accepted part of life. We get caught up in the demands of daily living, chasing success, and trying to meet everyone's expectations, which eventually leads to burnout. But the Bible offers us a path to peace, reminding us to cast our burdens on God and live intentionally.

In this chapter, we'll explore how to maintain balance and prevent stress while pursuing success, using both practical strategies and the timeless wisdom of scripture.

Understanding the Roots of Stress

Stress often stems from worrying about things beyond our control. It's easy to feel overwhelmed when life's uncertainties pile up. The Bible tells us: *"Do not be anxious about anything but in every situation, by prayer and petition, with thanksgiving, present your requests to God. And the peace of God, which transcends all understanding, will guard your hearts and your minds in Christ Jesus"* (Philippians 4:6-7, NIV). This verse is a reminder that God's peace is available when we surrender our worries to Him.

One of the first steps to managing stress is acknowledging where it's coming from. Is it the fear of not achieving enough? Is it trying to control every outcome? Once we identify the source, we can invite God into the situation and focus on what we can control—our response.

Leading Yourself with Peace and Intentionality

To avoid the trap of stress, we must learn to lead ourselves intentionally rather than let life happen to us. This requires self-awareness and setting boundaries. The Bible advises us to manage our lives well: *"Let all things be done decently and in order"* (1 Corinthians 14:40, KJV).

Practical Tip: Create Order to Avoid Overwhelm

- Take time each week to plan and organize. Create daily routines that help manage both your work and personal life.

- Set clear boundaries around your time, learning to say "no" when necessary, even to good things, so you don't take on more than you can handle.

Jesus modelled this when He withdrew to quiet places to pray, even when crowds sought Him: *"But Jesus often withdrew to lonely places and prayed"* (Luke 5:16, NIV). Taking time away from the chaos allows us to refuel and remain centred in God's peace.

Casting Your Worries on God

We often carry stress because we think we must figure everything out on our own. However, the Bible teaches us to cast our cares on God: *"Cast all your anxiety on Him because He cares for you"* (1 Peter 5:7, NIV). Trusting that God is in control helps release the pressure of trying to manage everything ourselves.

Practical Tip: Establish a Prayer Routine

- Develop a daily habit of prayer, where you intentionally hand over your concerns to God.

- Keep a journal where you can write down your worries and prayers, allowing you to release them from your mind and trust God's guidance.

Trusting God doesn't mean neglecting our responsibilities, but it shifts the burden from our shoulders to His. When we start our day with prayer and surrender, we are reminded that we are not walking this journey alone.

Finding Rest in God's Presence

Rest is a biblical principle that is essential to preventing stress. God created the Sabbath as a day of rest, not just as a rule, but as a gift to refresh and restore us: *"Come to me, all you who are weary and burdened, and I will give you rest"* (Matthew 11:28, NIV). Jesus invites us to find rest in Him, not just physical rest, but spiritual and emotional rejuvenation.

Practical Tip: Honor Your Rest

- Set aside time weekly for rest—whether it's a day off or even an afternoon—to disconnect from work and responsibilities.

- Incorporate moments of rest throughout your day, such as taking short breaks or spending time in nature to reflect on God's creation.

God commands us to rest, recognizing our need to recharge both physically and spiritually. By resting in Him, we refuel for the journey ahead, ensuring we don't reach a point of burnout.

Reframing Negative Thoughts

Our thoughts can easily spiral into negativity, which feeds into our stress. Proverbs 23:7 says, *"For as he thinks in his heart, so is he"* (KJV). What we meditate on shapes our reality. If we constantly think about stress, it will become our reality. Instead, we are encouraged to renew our minds and think about positive, life-giving things: *"Finally, brothers and sisters, whatever is true, whatever is noble, whatever is right, whatever is pure, whatever is lovely, whatever is admirable—if anything is excellent or praiseworthy—think about such things"* (Philippians 4:8, NIV).

Practical Tip: Reframe Your Thoughts

- Start a gratitude journal, listing things you're thankful for each day. This shifts your focus from stress to the blessings around you.

- Catch yourself when you begin to think negatively and consciously replace those thoughts with scriptures or positive affirmations.

Reframing your thoughts is one of the most powerful tools to guard your heart against stress. By training your mind to focus on God's goodness, you reduce the weight of negativity in your life.

Building a Community of Support

One of the greatest sources of stress is isolation. God did not design us to carry our burdens alone: *"Bear one another's burdens, and so fulfill the law of Christ"* (Galatians 6:2, ESV). Having a support system of trusted friends, mentors, or faith communities can help alleviate stress by sharing the load.

Practical Tip: Cultivate Strong Relationships

- Identify a few people you can trust and lean on for support. Be open and honest about your struggles with them.

- Make time for regular fellowship, whether that's attending church, joining a small group, or spending time with friends who lift you up.

By leaning on others and allowing them to support us, we lighten the emotional load and experience the joy of shared burdens.

Trusting God for Stress-Free Success

Stress may be an inevitable part of life, but it doesn't have to dominate us. When we lead ourselves with intentionality, surrender our worries to God, find rest in His presence, reframe our thoughts, and build strong support systems, we set ourselves up for success without sacrificing our well-being.

As Jesus reminds us, *"Therefore I tell you, do not worry about your life, what you will eat or drink; or about your body, what you will wear. Is not life more than food, and the body more than clothes?"* (Matthew 6:25, NIV). Success isn't about achieving more at the cost of our peace, but trusting that God has a plan, and resting in His guidance as we pursue our goals.

With faith and practical strategies, we can truly win without burning out, living a life that's fruitful, purposeful, and aligned with God's will.

CALL TO ACTION

Get your free 30 minute coaching session: https://calendly.com/mindy-coaching/30-minute-coaching-consult

About The Author

Mindy McManus is the innovative founder of Mindy's Executive Coaching, LLC, a leading provider of transformative coaching and consulting services for executives and leadership teams. With a strong foundation in leadership and organizational development, Mindy leverages her expertise to foster dynamic partnerships with clients, unlocking their innate potential and inspiring a profound sense of creativity, leadership, and determination.

Mindy's Executive Coaching has evolved to specialize in facilitating impactful retreats, workshops, and keynote addresses tailored for executive teams and organizations. Her approach integrates cutting-edge methodologies in leadership effectiveness, emotional intelligence, and agility, ensuring that each program is uniquely crafted to resonate with the specific needs of her clients.

At Mindy's Executive Coaching, we excel in translating complex leadership principles into actionable strategies that enhance personal and professional growth. By seamlessly blending business acumen with holistic coaching practices, Mindy and her team empower leaders to navigate transitions, prevent burnout, and achieve unparalleled success.

Contact Info

Mindy's Executive Coaching

www.mindyscoaching.com

mindy@mindycoaching.com

www.linkedin.com/in/mindymcmanus

Bibliography:

BibleGateway. (n.d.). *Galatians 6:2 (ESV)*. Retrieved from https://www.biblegateway.com

BibleGateway. (n.d.). *Luke 5:16 (NIV)*. Retrieved from https://www.biblegateway.com

BibleGateway. (n.d.). *Matthew 6:25 (NIV)*. Retrieved from https://www.biblegateway.com

BibleGateway. (n.d.). *Matthew 11:28 (NIV)*. Retrieved from https://www.biblegateway.com

BibleGateway. (n.d.). *Philippians 4:6-7 (NIV)*. Retrieved from https://www.biblegateway.com

BibleGateway. (n.d.). *Philippians 4:8 (NIV)*. Retrieved from https://www.biblegateway.com

BibleGateway. (n.d.). *Proverbs 23:7 (KJV)*. Retrieved from https://www.biblegateway.com

"We cannot change what we are not aware of, and once we are aware, we cannot help but change."
Sheryl Sandberg

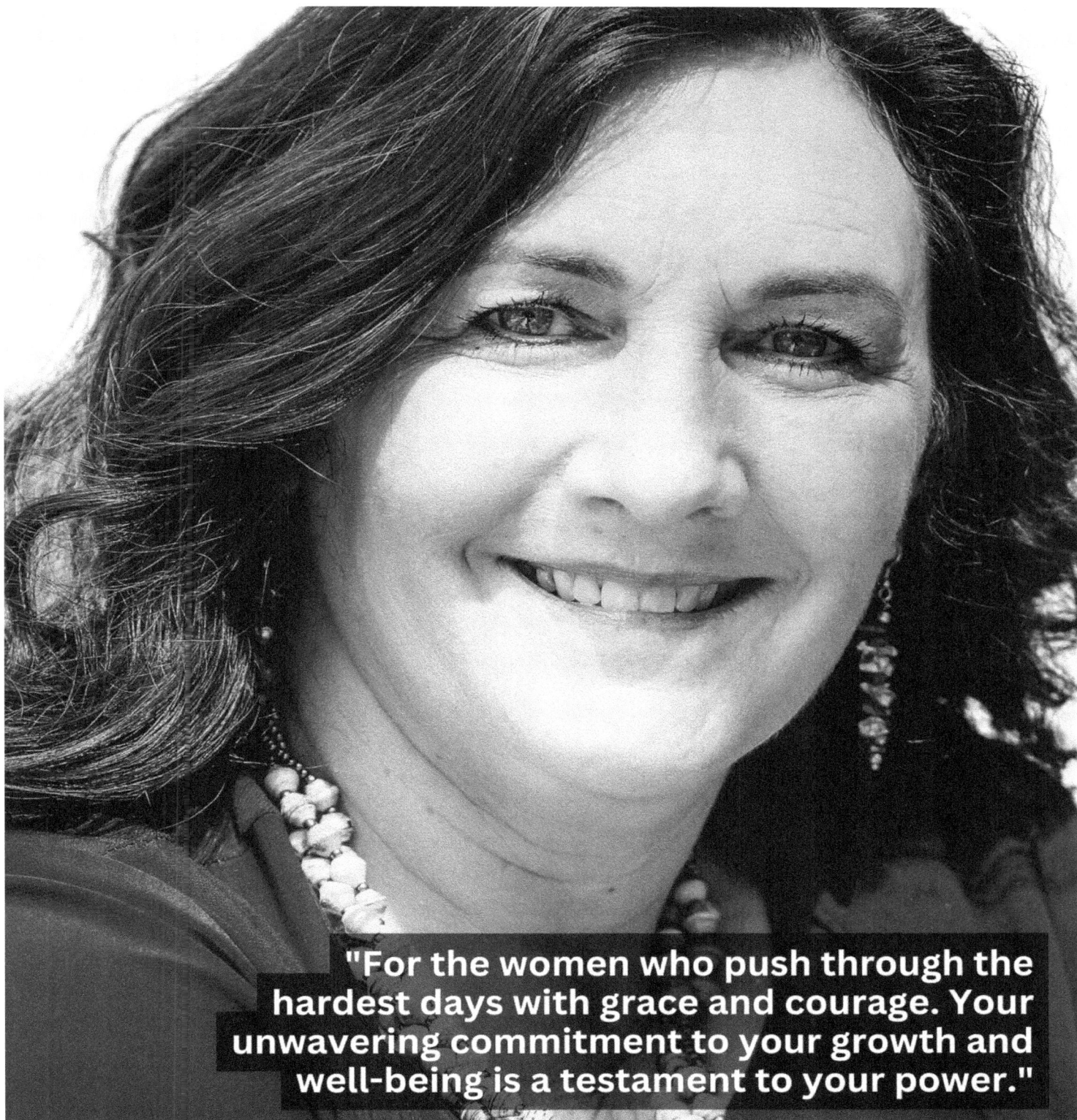

"For the women who push through the hardest days with grace and courage. Your unwavering commitment to your growth and well-being is a testament to your power."

ALIGNED FOR SUCCESS: ACHIEVING WEALTH AND WELLNESS WITHOUT BURNOUT

by Cheri Petroni

Chapter 8

Aligned for Success: Achieving Wealth and Wellness Without Burnout

by Cheri Petroni

S uccess can be costly. For purpose-driven women, the dream of achieving greatness while maintaining wellness and balance can feel elusive. We've been conditioned to believe that success requires endless hustle, long hours, and sacrifice.

What if I told you that you can align your energy, values, and purpose to create wealth, wellness, and success without all the exhaustion and burnout?

Well, you can! And it's easier than you think, once you reclaim your inner power and achieve alignment.

The Hidden Barriers to Alignment

Harmonizing our business and personal lives often clashes with our deep-rooted beliefs and past experiences. Many of us were raised with notions like

"Work hard, play later" or "Success requires sacrifice, while also being told, "You can have it all!"

Society reinforces these messages, leaving us with the impression that to succeed, we must constantly push ourselves beyond our limits. It's a lofty and unrealistic goal.

We wear multiple hats and are trying to "have it all". Do we really "want it all?" The fact is, most of us don't, and this programming subconsciously takes us down a path we didn't choose, creating habits and patterns that don't align with our values and desires. This misalignment with our true desires is the root of the hidden barriers that lead to overwhelm and burnout.

I was conditioned to embrace the grind. *"You can sleep when you're dead"* became my motto. I lived by it proudly. I pushed. I took on volunteer positions. I was the "YES!" person. I thought I had it all. Deep down, however, I felt disconnected from everything important.

Traditional career demands didn't align with my desire for freedom and balance. I was already losing sight of myself. I decided that owning a business was the answer. I could run the show.

"Boy was I wrong! I opened Oasis to Zen Transformation Spa. This brought less freedom! I was still tied to a 24/7 business. It worked me, rather than me working it."

I'm not alone in this struggle. Research shows that women in leaders experience burnout at higher rates than men. *A study by McKinsey & Company found that women in senior roles are 1.5 times more likely to feel burned out compared to their male counterparts.*

This is due not only to workplace pressures but also to managing family responsibilities and personal well-being. For many women, this misalignment manifests as chronic stress, fatigue, and a loss of purpose. We find ourselves working harder, playing less, and feeling increasingly unfulfilled.

We start to focus on what we didn't accomplish rather than our achievements. This striving for success is a sign that we feel "Not enough". We can't do it all, and inevitably we experience a motivation breakdown. And when we stay in this state, our bodies suffer.

Recognizing the Signs of Misalignment

The first step toward creating a life of prosperity without burnout is recognizing when we are out of alignment. Misalignment manifests physically, mentally, and emotionally, and the signs can creep up slowly.

Physically, we may experience fatigue, headaches, and other chronic health issues. Sleep is restless or nonexistent. Emotional eating or skipping meals is the norm, and we are too exhausted to exercise.

Mentally, we juggle multiple responsibilities and are overwhelmed. We lack clarity, passion, purpose, and motivation. We are on auto-pilot, yet overthink and doubt our choices.

Emotionally, we are disconnected from people, goals, and passion. We secretly want to run away. We feel irritable, impatient, and resentful, yet put on a "Happy Face" and pretend. Inside, we are unhappy.

Imagine a woman who wakes up exhausted before her day even begins. Her To-Do List is endless. She bounces between meetings, work, and family obligations.

She tells herself this is what success looks like, and underneath that, she knows something isn't right. She's headed for a breakdown if she isn't there already.

Statistics on burnout are alarming, particularly among women. *According to the World Health Organization, workplace burnout is now classified as a medical condition, with symptoms including energy depletion, mental distance from work, and reduced professional efficacy.*

Women often bear the majority of household and caregiving responsibilities and are particularly vulnerable to physical, mental, and emotional exhaustion.

Realigning Energy and Reclaiming Your Power

The good news is that realignment is possible. Through exploration and the right strategies, you can realign your energy and reclaim inner power. Harmony is about reconnecting with your core values, healing hidden barriers, and creating a lifestyle that honours both your ambitions and well-being.

I was shocked when I realized that I was not in harmony with my values. I had done everything "by the book," yet I wasn't making the money I deserved, my relationship was suffering, and I wasn't spending time where it mattered most. I was helping others create an aligned life, but I wasn't walking in my truth. I doubled down on longer hours and accomplished less and less.

I realized something had to change. I shifted my business model to include online services, focusing on coaching women to align their energies and build businesses that reflect their values without sacrificing personal fulfillment.

"One of the core principles we start with is clarity. Women must identify what truly matters to them; what they value personally and professionally."

What are you driven by? I'm driven by freedom, family, and fun. Living your core values will support the life and business you desire.

Here's a simple three-step framework to help you begin the realignment process:

Reconnect with Your Values: Reflect on what's most important. Write down your core values. Examine how they align with your current career and lifestyle. Are you honoring those values? If not, where can you adjust?

Heal Past Wounds: Misalignment is often rooted in unhealed emotional wounds. Acknowledge these traumas, whether from childhood or societal conditioning, and work to heal them. Reframe your limiting beliefs. Get support. You don't have to do this alone.

Implement Daily Practices: Realigning your energy requires consistent effort. Incorporate practices like meditation, journaling, or energy healing to stay connected to your purpose, maintain balance, and prevent burnout.

I've experienced first-hand how powerful these steps can be. A recent client came to me exhausted and ready to quit her business. She was successful by society's standards yet felt disconnected from everything. After implementing this framework, she connected with her family values, self-care, and a restructuring of her business. Once the patterns keeping her stuck were eliminated, she could reinvent and live a life of joy and purpose.

Mindset: The Key to True Alignment

At the heart of alignment is mindset. Our underlying old beliefs shaped our past and now our future. Clinging to childhood or societal beliefs and expectations will create misalignment, keeping us stuck in patterns we don't really want to live by.

Neuroscience confirms this: the brain's neural pathways form based on repeated thought patterns, meaning that unless we actively change our mindset as we grow, our brain will keep us in the same loop. Our brain basically needs a periodic upgrade like our computers.

According to research from Stanford University, neuroplasticity shows that the brain is highly adaptable and capable of rewiring itself based on new experiences and focused mental effort. This means that with the right mindset and habits, you can reshape your thoughts and behaviours to align with your goals.

This is why my coaching process is so successful. My **Personalized Freedom Plan** is rooted in these principles. It's simple, gentle, and based on the latest brain science. When we focus on shifting our mindset to align with what we want out of life. We break free from old patterns and rewire them into empowering ones. The brain believes what you tell it. Why not shift what you think and open doors to aligned fulfillment?

Sustainable Success Without Burnout

Once you align and clear patterns, your approach to success changes entirely. You no longer chase goals that leave you drained or unfulfilled. Instead, you create a business and lifestyle that nurtures you, one that is both financially rewarding and personally enriching.

Practical things that were difficult to maintain became easy, such as effective time management, self-care, and boundary setting. They are now part of aligned harmony.

A New Vision for Success

Imagine that same woman, now aligned. She wakes up each day energized and excited. She's built a business that reflects her values, with systems in place to support her goals. She rarely overextends herself. She has time for her family AND herself. Her career is thriving. Success, for her, is no longer elusive. She is living a life that is balanced, fulfilled, and aligned.

The journey to your greatest life may require effort, but it's one worth taking. By recognizing and overcoming unhealthy mindset patterns, you can create a new story of wealth, wellness, and success without compromise. As an **Aligned Woman,** you don't have to choose between success or well-being. You can have both, and I can support you along the way.

CALL TO ACTION

Your Earliest Core Wound: A Meditative Experience - https://oasistozen.com/meditative-experience

About The Author

Cheri Petroni is a mindset transformation leader, coach, and two-time bestselling author. She specializes in helping women and holistic business owners align their energy, clear inner blocks, and shift limiting beliefs to create a life and business that flows with purpose and joy.

With a background in education, Cheri spent years mentoring parents and students before embracing her entrepreneurial spirit by founding a successful holistic spa. However, the traditional brick-and-mortar business model did not align with her desire for freedom and balance. Raised with the belief that success required constant hard work and sacrifice, Cheri realized that true success didn't have to come at the expense of well-being or time with family.

Cheri transitioned into online coaching to gain the freedom to work from anywhere. Her programs focus on energy alignment, rewiring past programming, and clearing emotional blocks, allowing her clients to thrive without needing to constantly manage their businesses.

Today, Cheri enjoys the balance she has created—traveling, visiting her grandkids, and spending quality time with her husband—while continuing to help others build aligned, purposeful lives that offer both freedom and fulfillment.

Cheri Petroni holds an M.ED. with a concentration in early childhood development from the University of Nevada Las Vegas, as well as a multitude of certifications in holistic business coaching, wellness, and energy healing. She created Oasis to Zen Transformation Spa in 2014, where she started this transformational work, before expanding to the online community in 2017.

Contact Info

Oasis to Zen Transformation Spa

https://www.oasistozen.com

cheri@oasistozen.com

https://www.linkedin.com/in/cheripetroni/

References

1. **McKinsey & Company & LeanIn.Org. (2021). Women in the Workplace 2021.** https://leanin.org/women-in-the-workplace/

2. **https://www.who.int/mental_health/evidence/burn-out/en/World Health Organization (WHO). (2019). Burn-out an "occupational phenomenon": International Classification of Diseases.** https://www.who.int/mental_health/evidence/burn-out/en/

3. **Pew Research Center. (2015). Modern Parenthood: Roles of Moms and Dads Converge as They Balance Work and Family.** https://www.pewresearch.org/social-trends/2015/12/17/modern-parenthood

4. **Dweck, C. S. (2007). *Mindset: The New Psychology of Success.* Ballantine Books.**

"Don't be intimidated by what you don't know. That can be your greatest strength and ensure that you do things differently."

Sara Blakely

Part 2: Success

Success isn't just about reaching the finish line—it's about how you get there. You know what you're capable of, but the real question is: are you defining success in a way that aligns with *your* values and strengths?

For some of you, success is about bold moves and achieving big goals fast. You're driven by results and thrive on challenges. Others find success in precision and efficiency, knowing that every detail plays a role in the bigger picture. Some are motivated by the connections you build and the energy you bring to every interaction. Or maybe you're the reliable foundation "the rock", making sure that everyone and everything is aligned and on track.

No matter how you approach it, success isn't a one-size-fits-all journey.

You have the power to define it in a way that fuels your passion without draining your energy. It's about creating a path that feels right to you—a path that keeps you moving forward, confident, and fulfilled. In this section, we'll challenge the traditional definitions of success and empower you to build a version that suits *your* strengths and aspirations.

This is your moment to design success in a way that honours your unique style, keeps you thriving, and ensures you don't burn out along the way. Ready to claim your own version of success? Let's make it happen.

"To Matthias -- I love you more than Twentything!"

ORDINARY MOMENTS: KNOW YOUR VALUE

by Sallie Wagner

Chapter 9

Ordinary Moments: Know Your Value
#1 in a Series of Living Your Extraordinary Life

by Sallie Wagner

"Life changes fast. Life changes in the instant.
The ordinary instant." – Joan Didion

Life's moments can be absolutely extraordinary! Those anticipated events that we celebrate, both privately and with our communities – graduation, a new job, marriage, the birth of a child. But mostly life is made of ordinary moments. The 1,440 minutes that make up our days, broken down into smaller increments of moments and instants. Those moments that catch us unawares, which we deem to be extraordinary only in retrospect.

The ordinary moment in which you meet your true love for the first time. The ordinary moment of the sudden illness or injury, whether your own or of someone you love, extraordinary because of how completely it transforms your life.

How do we navigate the new path upon which those instants thrust us, while avoiding burnout, or perhaps healing from it? Interestingly, the cure is also the preventive. We can prevent and overcome burnout by recognizing and appreciating our own value.

When we know and step into our own value, we preserve ourselves in those moments. When we fail to recognize and appreciate our own value, we can easily slip into stress, burnout, and imbalance.

We've all heard that we teach people how to treat us. Most importantly, we teach ourselves how to treat ourselves. When we treat ourselves as unworthy by failing to recognize and appreciate our own value, we compensate by striving to obtain a false sense of value through hyperfocus and overachievement in our careers, our caretaker roles, or other endeavors in life. We seek confirmation of this false sense of value from the outside world rather than manifesting our true inner value outward to the world.

This focus on false value creates the vicious cycle of striving, yet never achieving. This cycle occurs because there's always more, always something else, that we need to achieve in order to feed the ravenous creature of our false sense

of value. This cycle is the epitome of burnout. And learning to appreciate and celebrate your inherent value is the cure that breaks the cycle.

One way to reconnect with our value and defeat burnout is by creating a sense of time abundance. Rather than focusing on the time poverty of 1,440 minutes each day, we embrace the abundance of time in our lives.

Where are you on this continuum from poverty to abundance?

Do you feel that your moments are crammed full with too much to do, and not enough time to do it? Days fly by and you wonder if you accomplished anything at all? You wish you could slow down or even . . . in the immortal words of Cher . . . turn back time?

"You're not alone."

Time abundance is a key topic of research for both economists and psychologists at top universities, including Yale, Harvard, Stanford, Warton, UC Berkeley, and UNC Chapel Hill. That's because our perception of time abundance v. time poverty has such a major influence on our productivity, efficiency, and effectiveness at work and in every other domain of life.

This research shows that time abundance is a leading predictor of every kind of wellbeing – physical, emotional, mental, and social – far more so than material affluence. And wellbeing is a contraindicator of burnout!

Further, those 4 areas of life – physical, emotional, mental, and social – are the key areas for building resilience, which is also a key indicator of overall wellbeing. People who live in time abundance experience less stress, more happiness, closer relationships, and better physical health than people who experience time poverty. All of which are antithetical to burnout.

"People who live in time abundance experience less stress,
more happiness, closer relationships…"

Certainly, objectively, we all know that each of us has the same 1,440 minutes each day, and despite whatever you may think about the nature of reality and the time-space continuum, we can't change that. At least, not yet! However, we CAN change our perception of those 1,440 minutes, and our PERCEPTION of time is what time abundance is all about. Your PERCEPTION will change as you leave time poverty behind and become your very own Time Lord, your very own Time Hero.

As a Time Hero, you'll become happier, healthier, more productive. You'll overcome and prevent burnout. You'll experience less chronic stress, which empowers you to spend more time pursuing your personal goals and dreams, improving your relationships, making more optimal choices about nutrition, exercise, leisure time . . . and all the rest!

Because, you see, as you start living in time abundance, you'll spend time more freely and generously with yourself – time really is just like money! In fact, economists recommend focusing first on increasing your time wealth rather than your monetary wealth if you want to have a better life.

Ironically, perhaps, time abundance doesn't correlate with how much free time you have. Studies show that most people who have lots of free time don't feel time rich – they just feel restless or bored. That's because time wealth isn't related to your schedule. Instead, it's determined by a range of physical, emotional, mental, and social habits and activities. In other words, it's determined by your resilience. It's determined by living out your values in a way that's consistent with your personal sense of value.

With some simple techniques that you can implement each day, you can create time abundance for yourself. You can heal from and prevent burnout. As you do so, you'll decrease your stress, and you'll be empowered to experience more happiness, closer relationships, and better physical health.

Let's look at 3 of those techniques.

First, an easy step you can take to start creating time abundance is to power up! It turns out that increasing your sense of personal power increases your perception of time abundance.

A fun way to increase your sense of your own personal power is to assume your power stance. We all have it – that power pose that we step into when we claim and ignite our sense of personal power. The (perhaps) guilty pleasure of your superhero pose. Your Time Hero pose!

When you increase your sense of your own personal power, you change your perception to one of increased time abundance. You pull yourself out of time poverty and step into time abundance.

Second, give your time away. It sounds like a paradox, counterintuitive. Yet, the research shows that when you give away just 10 minutes of your time by helping somebody else, it has the same effect as if you suddenly discovered that you got an hour of extra free time! Talk about ROI!

Third, add novelty to your day. Each day, do something new – learn a new word, try a new food, go somewhere you've never been before.

You might also do something familiar in a different way. Take a different route to work, or to do errands. Write with your non-dominant hand, brush your teeth with your non-dominant hand.

Experiment with anything that's new and different

Here's why novelty is effective in increasing time abundance. When you do something familiar, in the same familiar way, your brain uses less energy and works faster. That's because it's using familiar, well established neural pathways.

We've all experienced this . . . you take a shower, then afterward you're not sure whether you shampooed. You drive to the store, arrive there, and you realize you don't remember the actual journey.

You see, the faster your brain works – performing a familiar task in the same way – the faster we perceive that time flies. When your brain processes something quickly, you experience the event as happening quickly. In a weird twist, it appears the better you are at something, the more time poverty you may experience!

On the other hand, when you do something new, your brain works harder. That's because it's creating new neural pathways. Which means you spend more time processing the event, so you experience the event as happening more slowly. You're focused in the present. And you actually perceive time as passing more slowly!

That brings a whole new meaning and importance to being present.

With these simple steps, you can easily increase your wellbeing by building resilience, which increases your power and success! All of which cure and prevent burnout!

As you heal from and prevent burnout, you are able to embrace and enjoy those 1,440 minutes in your day, broken down into the smaller increments of moments and instants. The ordinary moments of life in which life truly happens.

You are free and empowered to pursue your career and other endeavors with joy. Free to embrace the honor and privilege of caring for a loved one. Empowered upon the Great Adventure, the Grand Experiment which is life. As you live out your Ordinary Moments in your Extraordinary Life!

Ready to experience even more time abundance? Please accept my gift to you...

CALL TO ACTION

Ordinary Moments: Know Your Value . . . Creating Time Abundance

And stay tuned for the next installment of Living Your Extraordinary Life! Complimentary eBook - https://salliewagner.my.canva.site/creating-time-abundance

About The Author

Sallie Wagner is a multiple #1 international best-selling author, sought after speaker, lawyer, real estate broker, and Life Alchemist!

Sallie deploys powerful transformation tools including Emotional Freedom Techniques, evolved Neurolinguistic Programming, and trauma-aware modalities to launch clients into action for rapid, concrete results. Clients reclaim the power of conscious choice in their lives and discover and live the life that makes them come alive!

Contact Info

Intentional Life Coaching

https://intentionallifecoaching.net/

swagner@salliewagnerenterprises.com

https://www.linkedin.com/in/sallieintentionallifecoaching/

> "To every free soul across the globe."

SUCCEED WITH HEART, NOT HEAT!

by Youssef Skalli

Chapter 10

Succeed with Heart, Not Heat!

by Youssef Skalli

still remember the heat rushing through my body, a fiery sensation that felt like my brain and heart were under siege. It wasn't just stress; it was the manifestation of deep exhaustion from years spent chasing *"success"* at all costs. It was the kind of heat that wasn't just the physical one which I ignored for years despite all the alerts my body was sending, it was an emotional heat, as if my body, my heart, and my brain formed a coalition to send me a strong message I could no longer ignore; "I had pushed too far."

It was on that October afternoon in a narrow gothic street in Barcelona - where I was living at the time- when I walked out of the psychologist's office, burnout diagnosis in hand with a medical leave that read "temporary disability for burnout, prolonged anxiety and symptoms of depression."

I found myself staring at emptiness while dragging my feet back home, feeling a heavy weight of guilt, exhaustion, and confusion. How did I get here? I loved my work, I had always believed in working hard, but this wasn't hard work;

this was a breakdown. That rush of heat was the wake-up call I needed. The cost of "*success*" had become too high.

"It was a moment that forced me to pause and ask:

Is this what success really looks like?"

My burnout journey was a pivotal shift in my life, allowing me to reconsider wholeheartedly everything I believed about achievement. It was clear: success, the way I had been pursuing it, was too expensive. I realized that I needed to redefine success, not as a measure of how much I could accomplish, but as a reflection of how fully I could live, work, and learn without losing my health, my heart, or myself in the process.

This realization transformed my approach to life and career, and it's at the heart of my passion and mission today to help others achieve their goals and aspirations, without sacrificing their well-being.

I am determined to help people succeed not by pushing harder but by listening more closely to their bodies, their emotions, and their true values. The pursuit of success should uplift you, not tear you apart.

An Invitation to reframe success:

Let me invite you to reflect on your own definition of success.

For so long, we've been conditioned to believe that success is about climbing ladders, gaining social validation, achieving milestones, and pushing ourselves to our limits… Does success have to be this relentless pursuit of "more"?

We conditioned ourselves to think of success in terms of external achievements; money, status, titles… What if success could be about balance, purpose, fulfillment, and living a life aligned with who you truly are?

I came to the conclusion that success, in its most sustainable form, is about building a life that reflects your heart's intentions, not just your perceived career demands. It's about living, working, and learning in a way that feels right to you, not what society expects. It's not just about *what* you do, but more importantly *why* and *how* you do it.

As you read this chapter, I invite you to rethink success from a holistic perspective, keeping in mind that success isn't a one-size-fits-all formula; it is as unique as you are. Consider how your success might look when it's not driven by heat, and it is guided by the heart.

The Power of Emotional Insights

One of the most powerful shifts in my burnout recovery was learning to tune into my emotions, what I call emotional insights or emotional self-influence.

Before my burnout, I used to see emotions as distractions. When I felt exhausted or overwhelmed, I ignored those feelings and just kept pushing.

Emotional Intelligence meant to me emotional control and oppression, I imposed on myself the pressure to maintain a "professional" façade by burying my emotions. But burnout taught me that emotions aren't weaknesses, they are informative messages and powerful teachers.

Your emotions are your body's way of telling you what's going on beneath the surface. Are you feeling constantly on edge? That might be a sign you're pushing too hard. Are you feeling unmotivated? That could be your mind's way of telling you to reassess your goals.

Learning to name, understand, and interpret my emotions has been a game-changer. It means being in tune with how you feel and making adjustments, not to avoid discomfort but to understand what your emotions are telling you. It's giving yourself the permission to feel, pause and ask, "What do I need right now?"

Your heart and mind are allies on this journey, not enemies. Success driven by emotional insights means sustainable success driven by heart.

The Adaptability Mindset: Navigating Change Without Losing Yourself

Adaptability is often praised as a key to success, but there's a hidden danger in how we might think about it. In the wrong context, adaptation can lead to burnout. Adjusting to unhealthy environments, toxic workloads, or unrealistic expectations without questioning whether it's sustainable.

The adaptability mindset I refer to is different. It's not about fitting yourself into damaging situations, but about staying flexible without losing yourself in the process. This means being open to change but always keeping your heart and values at the center of your decisions. It is nurturing the ability to shift your approach when faced with a new situation or when things don't go as planned. This does not mean adapting at all costs or losing yourself in the process. It means being flexible while staying grounded in your values. When something no longer aligns with who you are or threatens your well-being, adaptability also means knowing when to walk away.

True adaptability isn't about bending until you break; it's about developing an intentional balance between bending and binding. being resilient while maintaining your sense of self. It's about finding new ways to grow, but only in ways that are true to your heart and in alignment with your emotional wellness and long-term goals.

Values-Driven Self-Leadership: Leading from the Heart

At the core of sustainable success is the ability to lead yourself with intention, integrity, and purpose.

Burnout made me realize that I wasn't leading my own life, I was being led by external expectations. But once I reconnected with my core values, I began to lead from within, making decisions that aligned with what truly mattered to me.

Values-driven self-leadership is about knowing your deepest heart's intentions and letting those guide your choices. What matters most to you? What gives your life meaning? When you can answer these questions and live in alignment with your values, success becomes a byproduct of living authentically and intentionally.

Self-leadership isn't about doing more, it's about doing what's right for you. It's about developing a sense of agency in your own life, leading yourself in a way that honours your values, your wants, your needs, and your emotional well-being.

When you lead with your values, you create space for a life and career that reflects who you are, not who you are supposed or expected to be. And that, in itself, is the most empowering form of sustainable success.

Success is a Shared Journey: The importance of social support

One of the most profound realizations in my recovery journey was understanding the importance of social and professional support networks. People who want to see your success will help you succeed and celebrate with you.

"Success by heart is not a solo mission, it's shared with others who lift you up, celebrate your wins, and support you through setbacks".

It's also important to recognize that you don't have to carry all the weight yourself. Sometimes, we take on stress that doesn't even belong to us, whether it's from work, family, or external expectations. Learning to let go of unnecessary burdens and share responsibilities is essential for both mental clarity and emotional resilience. By leaning on trusted individuals, you create space to focus on what truly matters without being overwhelmed by decision fatigue or uncertainty.

Surround yourself with people who genuinely care about your success, not just your professional achievements but your personal success, your happiness, and your well-being. These are the people who will help you stay grounded and remind you that success is not about surviving. It's about thriving together.

Redefining Success with Heart

Burnout taught me that the path to success doesn't have to be a blazing, all-consuming fire. You can achieve incredible things without burning out. You can succeed with heart, not heat.

When you define success on your own terms, aligned with your values, driven by emotional insights, adaptable mindset, and supported by the right people, you create a life that's not only successful but sustainable. You don't have to sacrifice yourself to succeed. In fact, real success is living in a way that's true to yourself, your heart, and your well-being. **The choice is yours. Success, guided by heart, is yours to claim.**

CALL TO ACTION

30-minute Clarity Call: https://linktr.ee/myskalli

About The Author

Youssef is a Certified Values-Inspired Empowerment Coach, Organizational Development Practitioner, and professional workshop facilitator with over 20 years of leadership experience in multinational corporate environments.

After a successful career in Finance, Youssef transitioned to Human Resources, leading transformational projects across the globe. Now based in Ottawa, Canada, he founded SKALLIbility Coaching, a values-inspired practice built on Self-Knowledge-And-Living-Life-Intentionally (S.K.A.L.L.I.), and the practice of being G.R.E.A.T.: Grounded, Resilient, Empathetic, Aware, and Thankful.

Youssef is passionate about the power of Adaptability Mindset and thrives to empower individuals navigating life's transitions and executive mobility with resilience, purpose, and intentional values alignment.

Multilingual (English, French, Arabic, and Spanish), Youssef champions inclusivity, equity, and diversity with a passion for cultural humility. His approach combines career and life coaching, offering his coachees a holistic path to personal and professional success on their own terms.

After a burnout journey, Youssef became an active advocate for mental health and emotional wellbeing, he has co-authored, so far, three book anthologies on leadership and transformation ("Leadership Without Borders," "30 Days to Transformation," and "MidLife Without Crisis").

His social network calls him the "Smile Instigator," and his professional network refers to him as the "Emotional and Social Fitness Trainer," two titles that he welcomes with pride.

When he is not coaching, Youssef enjoys community volunteering, biking, hiking, fus on cooking, and creating short family videos.

#HumanUp #BeGREAT

Contact Info

SKALLIbility Coaching by Youssef Skalli

youssef@skallibility.com

https://www.linkedin.com/in/myskalli

FROM BURNOUT TO BLOSSOM

by Annie Izmirliyan

Chapter 11

From Burnout to Blossom

by Annie Izmirliyan

I sit back with awe and wonder at my life today – blessed with aligned community connections, financial opportunities and spiritual blessings. As a CEO of multiple businesses, an international speaker, a professional mentor and a mother extraordinaire, I never imagined that working in the wealth management world, including investment brokerages and insurance companies would lead to a fulfilling life. For the last 2 decades, I have helped thousands of individuals, families, and business owners with an in-depth understanding of what drives their financial planning goals and behaviours, with tangible step-by-step solutions and recommendations.

Since 2013, I have coached hundreds of advisors on how to build a practice of integrity through the use of financial planning and focusing on building genuine relationships with their clients. As a speaker and part-time professor of Financial Planning and Insurance, I have helped over 150 students (and counting) navigate a career in financial services in a relatable and collaborative way. Since 2021, I have hosted and organized a Mentorship Program for financial services professionals using tangible tools and assessments to understand their instinctive strengths to guide each person to become the person they were meant to become.

And yet, in 2020, I found myself thinking… "Oh no….not again. Not this tummy-twisting, mind-numbing, soul-sucking feeling…burnout!...Again?!" This feeling was starting to feel so common, that I had become comfortable in my own discomfort. The worst part of it was that I had such brain fog, I couldn't see that it was affecting my family as well.

I remember I had just started a new job in January 2020 and heard the magic words that most of the corporate world seems to value, "Welcome to your corner office". Wow, I thought. This is it! This is a huge career milestone in the corporate world, right? However, 2 months later we would all be told to go home due to a pandemic lockdown. Well, that didn't last long, I thought, but I'll be back soon. I can handle this, no problem. I'm adaptable and resourceful and I actually like working from home. What I didn't account for was that my unconscious feelings about not *being* enough would translate into unhealthy behaviours based on the feeling that I wasn't *doing* enough.

If you're a "Type A," hyper-independent, high-achieving person like me,
you know what I'm talking about.

In 2020, I was already a single divorced mom of a beautiful and smart 7-year-old little girl. I was also still recovering from cancer surgery years before, navigating a new corporate environment, studying for another designation, and coordinating visitation schedules. And NOW I was going to be homeschooling, coordinating Zoom schedules with the school, ensuring engagement and participation, and be fully accessible to another person who didn't understand the rules of corporate etiquette?! As I write this out, I realize how much this really was to deal with...and how little people knew about what I was going through. Because I was *so* used to handling everything by myself and wasn't used to asking for help.

When I look back, I realize I found some pretty creative ways to work through the burnout. In addition to thinking that this lockdown probably wouldn't last long, I deferred my vacation until later, and later. And later, my go-to solution for dealing with the burnout...was taking on new projects. Yes, you heard me. I couldn't deal with what was already on my plate, so I found new projects and initiatives to get excited about! Do you want to hear something even crazier? These new projects didn't even pay me. I worked on fumes... for free. What was I thinking?!

I remember when I heard the word "burnout" for the first time. Great, I thought, now we had a word that could describe everything...Why my chest felt tight more often than not, why my stomach was constantly in knots, and why my ability to care about "work performance" was at an all-time low. And while there were certainly discussions about the effects of mental health in the corporate environment, I didn't feel adequately supported. I was feeling depleted, discouraged and half-alive.

> *"I remember when I heard the word "burnout" for the first time. Great, I thought, now we had a word that could describe everything…"*

So, in June I made an executive decision. I decided to wander into technology for some relief, including Uber Eats, Instagram, and online dating. Ordering food with a couple of taps on my phone was fun and a bit of a lifesaver at times. Instagram was and still is a time-drainer but provided much-needed comic relief and education. And online dating….well, let's just say there were some interesting experiences, and it really was a full-time job by itself. All of these got me out of my bubble, so I suppose they were effective in that regard.

And yet, life kept spinning faster and faster… So, how did I think it was ok to spin further and further down the rabbit hole? Well, that's the problem. You lose clarity of mind and effective problem-solving when you're burned out. You're in survival mode, barely holding your head above water. I'd barely been surviving being a single parent with full-time custody of a young and energetic child with very little family support. Recovering from a serious surgery and trying to regulate my body was taking a toll on my stomach. And I felt like I was trying to support my daughter and the company I worked for while operating with a *leaky cup*.

You see… the truth about burnout for me was:

1) I was not operating in a role or environment that fulfilled me. In fact, when I told a supervisor that I was planning to change roles in 1 year, they begged me to stay and offered me more money. It was at that moment that I realized that even if I made more money the following year (and I was already making 6 figures), nothing would have changed.

2) I thought I was supposed to be better than Superwoman. I had, mistakenly, learned long ago that the job description for life was to be all things to all people. Oh! And never show others how much you're struggling. What a slippery slope that turned out to be.

3) Although I was happy to extend myself to help others, I didn't know how to ask for help or set boundaries on my time and energy. Who had time to ask for help?! I had to get things done and I was already behind!

These limiting beliefs and mindsets resulted in behaviors that became quite debilitating, quite quickly. So, how did I win big without losing myself?

Well….first, I had to find myself. It was time to build a new world and redefine the meaning of success. I knew that nothing would change if I didn't change anything.

I don't know about you, but I can be stubborn at times. (I can already see those closest to me giving me that look. The one that says, "Ya think?" while still loving me anyway.) So, I had to get out of my own way and consider *new* ways of solving old problems. More accurately, I had to give myself permission to take the time to figure out what was most important to me. It sounds really simple, but I already felt as if I never had enough time. So, I needed some reinforcements… I had to do something very foreign to me… I had to ask for help. At first, I felt so exhausted I couldn't even figure out what kind of help I needed. I just knew I needed it. I had to learn how to speak up in a way that respected me, the human being, not just the human doing.

What I didn't realize was that friends and colleagues were waiting for me to give them the opportunity to support me. They didn't always know what I needed, but they could see I was dealing with more than most and they really wanted to be there for me. And when I held back, they felt the pain of it too.

"It was like I was holding back a part of me, thinking

I was protecting everyone. Really, I was just building

my own prison of fear, shame and blame."

So, all I had to do was be open and vulnerable and, together, we could brainstorm solutions that respected both sides. I know what you're thinking… "Really Annie, is that all? Oh sure, let me just open up all my deepest fears and concerns and let those closest to me see what a fraud I really feel like." Or perhaps you're already thinking of all the ways they'll tell you how they CAN'T help you?

The thing is, they already see that you're struggling, possibly even suffering. AND they're still sticking by you. Why not give it a try? By opening up to those I trusted, the solutions were usually easier and simpler than what I had made it out to be in my head. Our bonds of friendship deepened as a result. And I learned to be compassionate with myself. I had to learn what it meant to rest… intentionally, and not because I was exhausted.

"This level of self-care became my superpower. I could now proactively

check in with my body, listen to what it needed and take action to honour it. I

learned to live 24 hours at a time."

And finally, I learned what my boundaries were. You see, anger and joy can be informative emotions. Anger tells you where you feel an injustice, and joy tells you what can fuel and propel your soul to its true purpose. It turns out, I needed help here too, as I learned to communicate with others what was okay and what was not. Sometimes "No" had to be enough for me.

Success is not just about how much money you make. Abundance and true prosperity are about mental peace, physical health and emotional wealth. Which surprise, surprise…also supports financial fulfillment. And as you master the mental chatter, tune into your body, and learn to build healthy, collaborative relationships, you'll find it easier to avoid the off-ramp to burnout and enjoy the journey to blossom-town.

CALL TO ACTION

Win a 1:1 Financial Confidence Empowerment Call with Annie:

https://form.jotform.com/PowerfulWomenToday/win-a-financial-confidence-empow

About The Author

With over 20 years of experience in wealth management, financial planning, and sales leadership, I am passionate about helping people achieve their financial and professional goals through the lens of soulful wisdom. As a CEO with my financial practice, I naturally consider all the what-if scenarios and potential solutions.

I've educated thousands of people and coached hundreds of Financial Advisors to plan for the worst, so you can live your best life. As a divorced single mother, I've learned that compassion and authenticity helps people navigate a transformational journey of financial empowerment with soulful wisdom. So, are you ready to blossom to your best life?

Contact Info

Annie Izmirliyan

www.annieizmirliyan.com

annieizmirliyan@gmail.com

https://www.linkedin.com/in/annieizmirliyan/

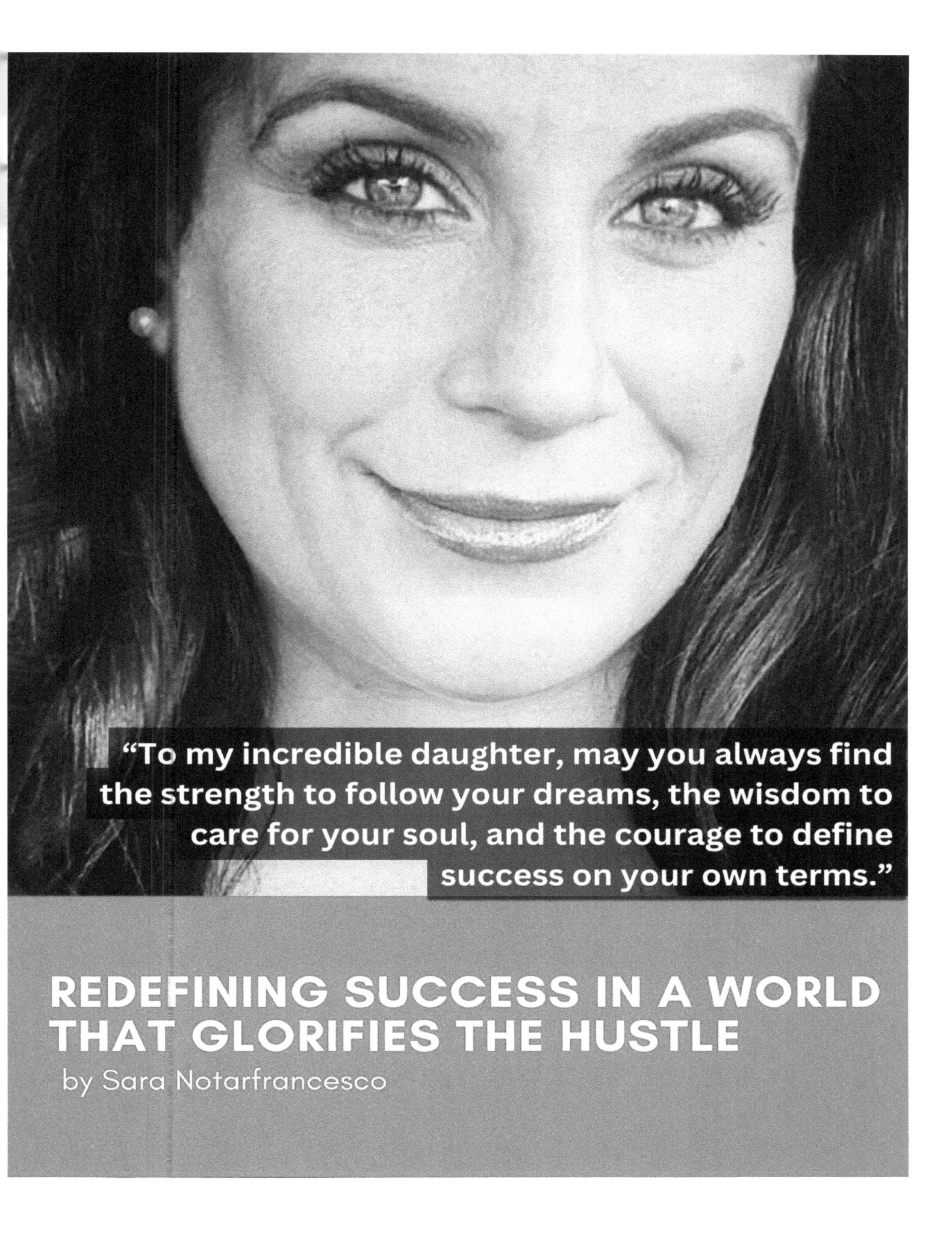

"To my incredible daughter, may you always find the strength to follow your dreams, the wisdom to care for your soul, and the courage to define success on your own terms."

REDEFINING SUCCESS IN A WORLD THAT GLORIFIES THE HUSTLE

by Sara Notarfrancesco

Chapter 12

Redefining Success in a World That
Glorifies the Hustle

by Sara Notarfrancesco

I n my journey, there have been countless times when things didn't go according to plan. Rather than seeing those moments as failures, I learned to view them as invitations to shift, to try a new approach, or to slow down. It's in those moments of adaptability that I've often found the most success—not by force, but by flow. It's a practice I encourage you to adopt. Allow yourself to shift when needed, and trust that your goals are still within reach, even if the path looks different than you initially envisioned.

How to Win Big Without Losing Yourself

It seems like every corner of the internet is preaching one message: hustle harder, work longer, grind until you get to the top. Ambition and drive are celebrated, but often at the expense of something critical—our health, happiness, and overall well-being. I've witnessed it firsthand, in myself and countless others: the pursuit of success without boundaries or balance. And as someone who is committed to excelling while prioritizing mental, emotional, and physical well-being, I can tell you there is a better way.

The concept of success doesn't need to come wrapped in exhaustion, stress, or burnout. In fact, it's possible to achieve your greatest goals and still feel connected to your core, without losing yourself in the process. It's all about working smarter, setting boundaries, and redefining what success means to you.

Redefining Success in a World That Glorifies the Hustle

We live in a culture that often glorifies the relentless hustle—the idea that success can only be achieved if you're constantly on the move, sacrificing your time, energy, and sometimes even your mental health. We've been told over and over that to make it to the top, we have to give up parts of ourselves, but that couldn't be further from the truth. The first step to success without burnout is realizing that you get to define what success looks like. It doesn't have to look like working 80 hours a week or skipping meals and self-care routines just to "get ahead." It can look like pursuing your goals while maintaining a life you love. It can be holistic, balanced, and joyful.

For me, the turning point came when I realized that burning out wasn't a badge of honor. In fact, it was a warning sign that I was pushing too hard and forgetting to take care of myself.

I learned that when I'm at my best—physically, mentally, emotionally—I'm more creative, more productive, and more effective. I can show up for my work in a way that feels aligned and purposeful, without sacrificing the things that matter most to me.

The Myth of the "Overnight Success"

We have all heard that success is not a sprint; it is a marathon. The truth is traditional timing isn't what matters. What truly counts is the effort, consistency, discipline, and belief in building a solid foundation. This takes time. Yes, there will be late nights and busy periods, but these shouldn't be the norm. We're allowed to pace ourselves; in fact, it's essential for the long term.

"The truth is traditional timing isn't what matters. What truly counts is the effort, consistency, discipline, and belief in building a solid foundation"

Over time, I learned that scaling back isn't a sign of weakness, it's a sign of wisdom. There is strength in knowing when to rest, reflect, and recharge. Often, it's in those moments of quiet that the biggest breakthroughs happen. Your mind needs space to breathe and wander, and your body needs time to restore its energy. When you give yourself permission to slow down, you actually set yourself up for greater success in the long run.

Practical Strategies for Winning Without Losing Yourself

So, how do you achieve your goals without sacrificing yourself along the way? Here are a few strategies that have helped me—and many others—find a more sustainable path to success.

1. **Set Clear Boundaries** Boundaries are non-negotiable when it comes to success without burnout. Know when to say no, even when it feels uncomfortable. Protect your time and energy as fiercely as you protect your goals. That might mean scheduling downtime on your calendar just like you would a meeting or turning off your phone after a certain hour to avoid unnecessary distractions.

It's easy to think you have to be available 24/7 to achieve greatness, but that's a myth. Productivity thrives within well-defined limits. When you give yourself permission to rest, you'll return to your work with renewed focus and creativity.

2. **Prioritize Self-Care** I know you've heard it before, but self-care really is a game-changer. It's not a luxury; it's a necessity. Success and self-care are not mutually exclusive—you can have both. Whether it's morning meditation, exercise, or simply taking time to read and unwind, find routines that help you recharge. Think of self-care as a way to fuel your success rather than detract from it.

The more I've leaned into this, the more I've realized that my best ideas come when I'm rested and well-taken care of. It's not about working harder; it's about working in alignment with your well-being.

3. **Delegate and Ask for Help** You don't have to do it all yourself. In fact, trying to do everything on your own is a recipe for burnout. Surround yourself with people who support your vision and can take on tasks that drain your energy or take time away from what you do best. Learning to delegate not only frees up your time, but it also allows you to focus on the work that inspires.

Asking for help is not a sign of weakness—it's a sign of strength and leadership. You don't need to be everything to everyone. Focus on what you excel at and bring in others to help you with the rest.

4. **Embrace the Journey** Remember why you started in the first place. Success is not just about the end goal, it's about the journey. If you're not finding joy in the process, it's time to reassess. What parts of your work bring you joy? For me, it is the purpose of supporting others in helping them see the beauty of their reflection in the mirror. What brings you fulfillment and excitement? Lean into those aspects and make them a bigger part of your day.

The grind can be grueling, but it doesn't have to be joyless. When you start to enjoy the process, you'll find that success follows naturally. The energy you bring to your work will be reflected in your results.

Embracing Balance for Lasting Success

Balance isn't just a buzzword—it's essential for long-term success. Without balance, you'll find yourself on a path to burnout, and the truth is, you can't pour from an empty cup. I've learned this the hard way, and my message is quite simple: Don't wait until you're burned out to make a change.

Take inventory of your life.

Are you spending your time on what matters most to you? Are you giving yourself the space to breathe and reflect? Are you showing up for your work in a way that feels authentic and aligned with who you are? If the answer is no, it's time to make adjustments.

"Real success isn't about pushing yourself to the brink—it's about finding a rhythm that allows you to thrive, both personally and professionally."

The Power of Being in Alignment

At the core of sustainable success is alignment—alignment with your values, your purpose, and your well-being. When you're aligned, success feels less like a struggle and more like a natural flow of energy. You're not fighting yourself; you're working with yourself to create something meaningful.

For me, alignment means checking in with myself regularly and asking: Does this feel good? Is this in line with my greater purpose? If the answer is no, I adjust.

Embracing Flexibility and Adaptability

Another key to success without burnout is the ability to remain flexible. Life happens, things change, and sometimes our plans need to be adjusted. That doesn't mean you've failed or that your goals aren't within reach. It simply means that you are adapting to the circumstances in front of you, and that's a strength, and most often times the exact reason you are changing to redirect yourself into alignment.

I used to be the type of person who needed everything to go exactly as planned. I thrived on routine and control. But I realized that such rigidity stifles growth. When you cling too tightly to one way of doing things, you limit your ability to see new opportunities or make adjustments when necessary. Flexibility allows you to stay grounded while navigating life's inevitable challenges with grace and resilience.

The Importance of Rest and Recovery

Rest is not just a luxury; it's a necessity for high achievers. Yet, in the hustle culture, rest is often portrayed as something only the weak or unmotivated indulge in. I'm here to tell you that's a myth—and a dangerous one at that.

True success doesn't come from constant motion. It comes from knowing when to step back, recharge, and return stronger. We often think of recovery as something we do after we've burned ourselves out, but what if we started to view rest as part of the process? What if we made recovery a regular part of our schedule, just like meetings and deadlines?

"True success doesn't come from constant motion. It comes from knowing when to step back, recharge, and return stronger."

Incorporating rest into your routine is one of the most powerful ways to ensure you don't burn out. Whether it's taking a day off to unplug from technology, indulging in a creative hobby that fuels your soul, or simply getting enough sleep each night, recovery is essential to long-term success. When you honour your need for rest, you allow yourself to show up fully—recharged, creative, and ready to tackle challenges with clarity.

Personally, I've found that my best ideas often come after periods of rest, not during times of overwork. When I give myself the space to step away from the grind, I return to my work with fresh perspectives and renewed energy. It's like hitting the reset button, and it makes all the difference.

Celebrating Small Wins Along the Way

In our quest for success, we often get so focused on the end goal that we forget to celebrate the milestones along the way. But it's those small wins that keep us motivated, that remind us we're making progress, and that success is not just a future destination—it's something we're building every day.

Take the time to acknowledge your achievements, no matter how small they may seem. Did you complete a project ahead of schedule? Celebrate it. Did you manage to carve out time for self-care in a busy week? That's a win. Did you finally say no to a request that would have drained your energy? Applaud yourself for setting that boundary.

Success is not just about the big, flashy moments—it's about the accumulation of small, intentional steps. When you start to celebrate those steps, you reinforce the belief that you are on the right path. You create momentum, and that momentum is what will carry you forward.

I've learned to celebrate everything, even the things that might seem insignificant to others, because I know that each step I take is bringing me closer to my goals. It's a mindset shift that turns the journey into something joyful, rather than something burdensome.

Giving Yourself Grace

At the end of the day, the most important lesson I've learned on my journey to success is to give myself grace. We live in a world that often tells us we need to be perfect, to have it all figured out, and to never make mistakes. But perfection is an illusion, and striving for it only leads to frustration and burnout.

Give yourself permission to be human. Understand that you will have off days, that you might stumble, and that's okay. Success is not about being perfect; it's about being resilient. It's about getting back up when things don't go as planned and continuing to move forward with intention.

When I started giving myself grace, I found that my productivity actually improved. I was no longer paralyzed by the fear of making mistakes, and I allowed myself to learn and grow along the way. The pressure lifted, and I became more present in my work and in my life.

You are allowed to evolve. You are allowed to take your time. You are allowed to be both a work in progress and a success story at the same time. So, give yourself grace and keep going.

Final Thoughts: Success on Your Own Terms

Success without burnout is possible. It requires a shift in mindset, a willingness to prioritize your well-being, and the courage to redefine what success looks like for you. You don't have to sacrifice your health, happiness, or sense of self to win big. You can achieve your greatest goals while maintaining balance, joy, and fulfillment.

Remember, success is not just about the destination—it's about the journey. It's about showing up for yourself, setting boundaries, prioritizing rest, and celebrating the small wins along the way. It's about building a life that feels good from the inside out, not just one that looks good in the highlight reel.

So, as you continue on your path to success, I encourage you to take these lessons to heart. Embrace a new way of working—one that honors your well-being and allows you to win big without losing yourself in the process. Success, after all, should feel as good as it looks.

CALL TO ACTION
Connect with Sara on Instagram: https://www.instagram.com/saranotar_mua/

About The Author

Sara is an entrepreneur, beauty expert, and empathetic leader with over 15 years of experience in luxury skincare and makeup industries. Having worked with prestigious brands like NARS, Bobbi Brown, Origins, CHANEL, Giorgio Armani Beauty, Bumble and Bumble, and Smashbox, she brings a wealth of knowledge and a refined eye for beauty and transformation.

As the founder of Mirror & Mind, Sara has created a high-end coaching service designed to help individuals break free from self-doubt and limiting beliefs, guiding them toward self-love, empowerment, and personal transformation. By blending her beauty industry background with a holistic approach to personal growth, she supports clients in aligning their inner and outer radiance, helping them see their true potential.

Known for her empathetic leadership, Sara fosters a judgment-free, empowering space where clients can explore their personal growth with compassion and encouragement. Her approach emphasizes the importance of mental health, authenticity, and self-awareness, driving meaningful change in both personal and professional spheres.

In addition to her business ventures, Sara is a devoted mother and a resilient advocate for empowering others to discover their path to self-love and holistic wellness. Through her work, she inspires others to embrace their journey, achieve personal breakthroughs, and realize their full potential.

Contact Info

Mirror & Mind- Reclaim your Reflection & Embrace your Power

mirrorandmind@gmail.com

http://linkedin.com/in/sara-notarfrancesco

"For my daughter, Valentina."

HEALING AND BRIDGING THE GENERATIONAL GAP FOR SECOND GENERATION ASIAN WOMAN

by Lisa Li

Chapter 13

Healing and Bridging the Generational Gap for Second Generation Asian Women

by Lisa Li

Second generation Asian American women grapple with conflicts related to their identity and cultural background, in the dynamic Western society of today's era where East meets West and traditions collide with modernity. Feeling a sense of unease from not belonging in either realm and facing hurdles on their journey toward self-realization may lead to emotions of alienation and burnout. The section explores how Asian women navigate a generation divide aiming to blend traditions, with growth, for achievement without compromising their welfare.

Navigating the demands of family and society as Asian American women can be quite complex, at times. It's important to work towards healing and fostering connection between generations within Asian families in North America. This involves addressing the difficulties that arise when trying to harmonize values with influences. The aim is to promote conversations that reduce misunderstandings and emot onal strain caused by expectations and duties. These conversations can help second generation Asian women in finding a balance between their roots and personal aspirations without feeling conflicted, within themselves. By promoting empathy and fostering understanding, within the family unit strengthens bonds. Makes it easier to follow traditions, without feeling constrained by them.

The ultimate outcome of this healing journey is an atmosphere where everyone can thrive while also preserving their roots in a way

that resonates with future generations.

By bridging the gap and resolving issues within them, 2nd generation Asian women have the ability to regain authority, over their lives and create boundaries that promote wellness while pursuing a career and lifestyle aligned with their values and aspirations— all without the burden of guilt, from disappointing family or neglectful mindfulness practices. This journey also leads to a sense of identity where cultural heritage and individuality are valued without clashing against each other.

Many second-generation Asian women face professional challenges as they navigate the complexities of balancing two cultures and the conflicting desires of their families with their own dreams and goals. This struggle can lead to increased strain within family dynamics and a profound internal conflict if not addressed effectively.

This stress frequently manifests in workloads as individuals attempt to handle all their responsibilities while reluctantly striving to meet both family expectations and personal career goals. The desire to succeed often leads to exhaustion when achieving outwardly is not accompanied by a sense of inner satisfaction. Success often impacts their being negatively and establishes a detrimental cycle of stress that is challenging to escape from.

In the worst-case scenario this unaddressed disparity between two realms could potentially result in crises, similar to anxiety and depression. Close family bonds that were meant to provide comfort and support may face strain or irreparable damage resulting in relationships that are challenging to mend.

Additionally, there's a concern about losing one's sense of self in this battle. Consistently prioritizing the happiness of others. Be it family friends or societal norms. Without taking into account one's desires can weaken self-assurance and blur identity. Consequently, the ongoing strain may pave the way for lasting discontentment as individuals find themselves living a life that seems insincere and detached from their selves. When all these different experiences come together like that the result is that it makes the person feel disillusioned and eager to find something that will help them discover who they really are.

"Consistently prioritizing the happiness of others. Be it family friends or societal norms. Without taking into account one's desires can weaken self-assurance and blurred identity."

Currently, many second-generation Asian women attempt to balance roles by working excessively hard and failing to fully meet expectations, in both aspects of their lives. They often struggle to establish boundaries at home and work while trying to excel in their responsibilities as a mother or daughter while also maintaining an image in the workplace. They consistently finish tasks promptly and are given more work as a reward, without hesitation when tasks are finished early; they remain silent, in the face of challenges. They readily assist their teammates whenever necessary while others might overextend themselves and work excessively in their professions to demonstrate their value or take up additional family duties to assuage feelings of guilt.

Many people seek traditional avenues, such as validation through achievements such as higher education and promotions to prove to their families that their decisions are valid and successful which often leads to acceptance, from others well as loved ones. Some individuals opt for counseling sessions and expert guidance to support their health and emotional stability while managing these pressures. There are those who seek solace in alcohol to cope with the stress of juggling responsibilities in life.

Though these approaches may provide respite at glance, in the grand scheme of things they are simply not sustainable over the long haul. Attempting to bear the burden of everything for the sake of others inevitably culminates in burnout. Living this 'double life' ultimately causes a fragmentation of identity as the constant back and forth demands mental and emotional exertion. Overcompensating in one sphere of life only ramps up the pressure over time, and career success alone cannot bridge the deeper emotional divide. Therapy and coaching can provide relief for symptoms, yet they may not address the issues that allow intercultural trauma to persist across generations. Additionally, alcohol consumption can lead to health problems that can be detrimental to overall health over time.

When the gap, between generations is resolved and connections are made stronger, second-generation Asian women will find peace and confidence within themselves. They can embrace their heritage while pursuing their dreams, avoiding the struggle of choosing one over the other. This blending allows for bonds with family built on respect and understanding rather, than duty or pressure. They will have the opportunity to guide their children with care and affection as they nurture the generation in an environment that promotes safety and growth.

"When the gap, between generations is resolved and connections are made stronger, second-generation Asian women will find peace and confidence within themselves."

Th s experience helps them embrace their goals and background in a way that blends smoothly without causing any tension or discordance between them both. It also opens doors for leadership roles which can lead to a professional life and opportunities for creativity that can bring about greater contentment. Moreover, redefining success to include self-care, happiness and personal fulfillment empowers these women to live confidently thus allowing them freedom to pursue their dreams and cultivate a sense of self.

Connecting the generations and facing the scars left by experiences shaped during our early childhood involves a mix of empathy and self-improvement, engaging in meaningful dialogues and introspection to redefine your own unique definition of achievement.

To start with the process that involves recognizing and honoring the emotions connected to those traumas which then allows for self-examination and contemplation.

1. **Leading with compassion** – speak openly with the goal to understand the mindset of the previous generations, with family members can aid in comprehension of behavioral patterns and empathy, building efforts that are essential in bridging the gaps between generations

2. **Seeking support** from professionals like therapists who are attuned to nuances that can offer personalized guidance and coping mechanisms based on individual journeys.

3. **Engaging in self-care** practices and mindfulness methods, like meditating, ground, and nature walks can bring you back to your center, enhance strength and overall wellness.

4. **Participating in community** activities and expressing creativity can also aid in reconnecting with roots. Nurturing a feeling of belonging.

5. **Establishing objective**s that resonate with values and dreams offers a positive outlook for the future empowering people to overcome previous hardships and build a satisfying existence.

Strengthening connections and promoting reconciliation across generations, empowers an entire generation of Asian women by freeing them from pressure and standards that could cause exhaustion and burnout. It also paves the way to create opportunities for positive transformations to spread across society at large. When these women embrace their strength and true selves they serve as role models, for future generations by demonstrating how to manage societal expectations while prioritizing self-care and self-love successfully.

This shift also brings about an influence on their families well. When family members see their daughters, sisters or cousins thriving while still maintaining their values respectfully it fosters communication, understanding and acceptance across generations. This contributes to the safety and success of the family by setting a precedent, for balanced women.

The healing process, for trauma among Asian American women and their community can start to unfold through the application of these solutions and bridge the divides between different age groups gradually. By adopting this

approach of fostering understanding and respect while empowering individuals

to embrace their selves fully, a vibrant and nurturing environment can be

nurtured within families, for the well-being of all members.

CALL TO ACTION
Schedule a 1:1 with me on how you can heal and achieve abundance through self-love: https://www.linkedin.com/in/lisa-l-370688126

About The Author
Born and raised in Canada in a traditional Asian household, I often felt like an outsider, navigating the complexities of my identity while searching for my place in the world. This journey has fueled my passion for helping others and making a positive impact on the lives of those around me. My love for the arts has always been a guiding force, inspiring me to express my thoughts and feelings creatively.

As a devoted mom to a joyful daughter and a grateful wife to a supportive husband, my family is my greatest source of inspiration. While free time is scarce, I cherish moments spent meditating and exploring nature through long walks, allowing me to recharge and connect with my inner self.

Through my writing, I hope to share my experiences and insights, fostering understanding and connection within our diverse communities. I believe in the power of empathy and conversation to bridge generational gaps, and I strive to inspire others to embrace their unique journeys.

Contact Info

Lisa Li

lisa@virtueharmonyplus.com

https://www.linkedin.com/in/lisa-l-370688126

"You have been assigned this
mountain to show others
it can be moved."
Mel Robbins

Part 3: Leadership

Leadership isn't just a title granted—it's a way of showing up. It's how you inspire, influence, and guide others toward a vision that matters.

Here's the truth: leadership looks different for everyone. Some are natural trailblazers, leading from the front with bold, decisive action. You thrive in high-stakes situations and push the boundaries to get things done. Others lead through careful planning and expert execution, ensuring every move is strategic and well thought out. Maybe your strength lies in motivating and energizing your team, bringing people together with passion and charisma. Or perhaps you lead by creating stability and trust, offering unwavering support and calm in every storm.

No matter your approach, true leadership means leveraging your strengths while staying connected to your well-being. It's not about fitting into a rigid mold—it's about embracing the kind of leader *you* are and making an impact without losing yourself in the process.

> **"Lead with intention, empowering others**
>
> **while staying empowered yourself."**

In this section, we'll explore how to lead with intention, how to empower others while staying empowered yourself, and how to create success without burnout. You'll learn how to step into leadership that feels authentic, sustainable, and aligned with your values.

This is your opportunity to lead with purpose, power, and the confidence that you can drive success without sacrificing yourself. Ready to unlock the leader within? Let's dive in!

"A life with deep relationships, a caring husband, sons and many grandchildren help you keep things in perspective. They are all a blessing every day. This chapter is dedicated my husband and our children. "

ACHIEVING YOUR GOALS WITHOUT LOSING YOURSELF

by Judy Cirullo

Chapter 14

Achieving Your Goals Without Losing Yourself

by Judy Cirullo

Success drives our current world and burnout has become an all-too-familiar experience for many ambitious professionals. The pressure to achieve more, work harder, and keep pushing forward has taken a toll on countless individuals across industries. Whether you're an entrepreneur, a corporate executive, or someone climbing the ladder in your career, the relentless pursuit of success can sometimes feel like a double-edged sword. We're told that to succeed, we must give it everything—our time, energy, and even our mental and physical health. But what if there were a way to win big without losing yourself in the process?

What if success didn't have to come at the cost of burnout, exhaustion, and overwhelm? Burnout, though prevalent, can be understood, prevented, and reversed. This chapter seeks to offer practical strategies to help you achieve your goals while maintaining your well-being.

My hope is that this chapter will serve as your guide to identifying the signs of burnout, understanding its root causes, and applying actionable solutions to strike a balance between ambition and self-care. You will learn how to approach your work with a mindset that values sustainable success—where you can reach your highest potential without sacrificing your health, happiness, or sense of purpose.

Understanding the Three Hallmarks of Burnout

In order to be proactive about mitigating burnout it is important to understand the 3 hallmarks of burnout and how they differ from overwhelm or other feelings of being stressed. Burnout is not just about feeling tired or stressed after a long day. It's a deeper, more insidious condition that can erode your motivation, passion, and effectiveness. To combat burnout effectively, it's crucial to understand its three primary indicators, or "hallmarks":

1. **Emotional Exhaustion**: This is the *overwhelming feeling of being drained, both physically and emotionally.* It manifests as chronic fatigue, a sense of depletion that isn't remedied by a good night's sleep or a weekend off. Emotional exhaustion arises from constant pressure, excessive workload,

and the sense that there's no end in sight. Over time, it can lead to feelings of helplessness and disillusionment. Loss of sense of connection to purpose.

2. **Depersonalization**: This hallmark refers to a *sense of detachment* or disconnection from your work, colleagues, or even your own goals. You might find yourself becoming increasingly *cynical, disengaged, or indifferent*. The work that once excited you now feels like a burden, and you may even start questioning why you pursued it in the first place.

3. **Reduced Sense of Personal Accomplishment**: Burnout can make you feel like you're no longer effective or capable in your role. You might begin to doubt your abilities or feel like your work lacks meaning, no matter how much effort you put in. This *erosion of self-efficacy* can sap your confidence and motivation, leading to a downward spiral of dissatisfaction and frustration.

Recognizing these three hallmarks of burnout is the ***first step toward addressing it***. If you find yourself experiencing one or more of these symptoms, it's a clear signal that something needs to change. Burnout doesn't mean you're weak or that you lack the stamina to succeed—it's a natural response to prolonged, unrelenting stress. And the good news is, it's reversible.

The Six Top Causes of Burnout for Ambitious Professionals

While burnout is often seen as an individual problem, its roots often lie in external factors related to how we work and the environments in which we operate. Understanding these causes is key to addressing burnout at its core. The *six most common causes of burnout* for ambitious professionals are:

1. **Work Overload**: One of the most significant contributors to burnout is simply having too much to do. When you're constantly juggling deadlines, responsibilities, and projects, it can feel like there's no space to breathe. The "always-on" culture, where success is often equated with constant hustle, pushes many professionals into overload, leading to exhaustion and burnout.

2. **Lack of Control**: Having little to no control over your workload, schedule, or decision-making process can lead to feelings of frustration and powerlessness. *Autonomy is a crucial factor in job satisfaction*, and when it's absent, it can significantly contribute to burnout.

3. **Insufficient Reward**: Rewards are not just about financial compensation—they include recognition, appreciation, and a sense of accomplishment. When professionals feel that their *hard work goes unnoticed or unappreciated, it can lead to resentment and burnout*.

4. **Breakdown in Relationships**: Isolation, poor communication, or a lack of supportive relationships can contribute to feelings of alienation. Whether you're working in a team or running your own business, the absence of a strong support system can make challenges feel overwhelming. *Human connections are vital to resilience,* and their absence makes burnout more likely.

5. **Unfair Treatment**: When people *feel they are being treated unfairly*, whether due to bias, favoritism, or inequity in workload distribution, it can *spark frustration and burnout*. Ambitious professionals, in particular, may feel this more than others, especially when recognition is absent.

6. **Misalignment of Values**: *Burnout is more likely when your personal values conflict with the expectations of your work or profession*. For example, if you are in a rigid work environment that impedes your creativity or value at work this can lead to significant stress and burnout.

By identifying these six causes, you can begin to take proactive steps to address the root issues contributing to burnout in your life. The key is to look at both your internal mindset and the external conditions shaping your work environment.

Assessing Burnout: A Tool for Self-Reflection

One of the ***most important steps in combating burnout is self-awareness***. By assessing where you are on the burnout spectrum, you can gain clarity on whether burnout is starting to creep in or has already taken hold. ***Self-reflection is the foundation for change***. The next section will introduce a simple self-assessment tool to help you gauge your current state of well-being.

Start by asking yourself the following questions:

- Do you feel physically or emotionally exhausted, even after periods of rest?

- Are you becoming cynical, disengaged, or indifferent toward your work?

- Do you feel like you're no longer as effective or accomplished as you used to be?

- Are you constantly overwhelmed by your workload or responsibilities?

- Do you feel a lack of control or autonomy in your professional life?

- Have you noticed a decline in the quality of your relationships with colleagues or clients?

- Are you experiencing frustration or resentment due to a lack of recognition or reward?

These questions are designed to help you reflect on whether burnout is affecting your performance, motivation, and overall well-being. If you find yourself answering "yes" to several of these questions, it's a sign that you may be at risk for—or already experiencing—burnout.

Once you've identified that burnout is present, ***the next step*** is to reflect and ask yourself what needs to change. This might involve shifting priorities, delegating tasks, or implementing more self-care. The goal is to recognize the warning signs early and take proactive steps to regain control and balance.

Strategies to Reduce and Reverse Burnout

Now that you understand the causes and signs of burnout, it's time to explore practical strategies to prevent and reverse it.

1. Set Boundaries to Protect Your Energy

Establishing boundaries is one of the most effective ways to prevent burnout. This might mean setting clear limits on your work hours, learning to say "no" to non-essential tasks, or creating designated time for rest and recovery. Boundaries help protect your energy and ensure that you're not constantly overextending yourself.

2. Cultivate Autonomy

One of the key contributors to burnout is feeling a lack of control. Whenever possible, seek ways to increase your autonomy in your work. This could mean taking more ownership of projects, negotiating for more flexibility in your schedule, or advocating for more decision-making power. The more control you have over your workload, the less likely you are to feel overwhelmed.

3. Prioritize Rest and Recovery

Success doesn't come from relentless hustle; it comes from sustainable effort. Prioritize rest and recovery just as much as you prioritize work. This includes not only getting adequate sleep but also incorporating activities that rejuvenate you—whether that's spending time in nature, practicing mindfulness, or engaging in creative hobbies.

4. Build a Support System

Success is not a solo endeavor. Building a strong support system of mentors, colleagues, or friends can help you navigate challenges, share the load, and provide emotional support. Surround yourself with people who understand your goals and encourage your balance and self-care.

5. Recognize and Celebrate Achievements

In the pursuit of ambitious goals, it's easy to overlook the progress you've made. Take time to celebrate your accomplishments, both big and small. Recognizing your achievements can boost your sense of personal accomplishment and motivate you to continue striving for success without burnout.

Redefining Success for a Balanced Life

Burnout is not a sign that you're doing something wrong—it's often the result of trying to do too much, too fast, for too long. By understanding the signs and causes of burnout, and by implementing these strategies, you can redefine what it means to succeed but not at the cost of your well-being. But instead, where you achieve your success while maintaining your health, happiness, and sense of purpose.

As you move forward, remember that success without burnout is not only possible but essential. You can win big without losing yourself in the process.

CALL TO ACTION

Discover your Driver and how it helps mitigate burnout: https://go.growstrongteams.com/why-discovery-offer

About The Author

Judy is a seasoned business owner, former clinician, and certified professional coach (CPC) with 40 years of experience. Having successfully managed 4 businesses across different states, she understands the challenges of leading and developing teams. Certified by the International Coach Federation (ICF) and trained in Conversational Intelligence (C-IQ), she is dedicated to helping leaders and teams create a culture of growth, development, and work-life balance. Her 6 Step People First Culture Framework empowers leaders to grow and develop their most valuable asset effectively - their people - and create balanced work environments that drive success. Much of her work begins with seasoned leaders and business owners with many years of experience who would like to explore how they can make a shift but continue to make a difference in the lives of others.

Contact Info

Grow Strong Teams

https://growstrongteams.com/

judy@growstrongteams.com

https://www.linkedin.com/in/judycirullo/

"Being able to put your blinders on and follow your intuition is what's validating."

Whitney Wolfe Herd

"To my Husband, Doug, family friends and colleagues"

RE-IGNITING YOUR CAREER WITHOUT BURN-OUT FOR WOMEN 45+

by Dr. Patricia. Suggs

Chapter 15

Re-Igniting Your Career Without
Burnout for Women 45+

Dr. Patricia Suggs

Let's begin with a story:

Sarah had always been a go-getter. By her mid-40s, she'd built a successful marketing career, raised two kids, and juggled family life with work. But as she hit 45, something changed. The long hours, endless emails, and constant pressure started taking a toll. Sarah felt exhausted—mentally and physically.

One afternoon, after yet another missed family dinner, she realized she needed to redefine what success meant. Sarah had spent years chasing promotions, believing that each new title would bring the satisfaction she craved. But the joy of each achievement was fleeting. It was time for a new approach.

Sarah negotiated a flexible work schedule, cutting back to four days a week. She stopped chasing every opportunity and instead focused on leading meaningful projects that aligned with her strengths. This shift allowed her to mentor younger colleagues, which brought her immense fulfillment.

With her newfound free time, Sarah rediscovered painting—a hobby she hadn't touched since college. It gave her a sense of calm and creativity she hadn't felt in years. Most importantly, she could now be present with her family, sharing meals and laughter that had been missing for so long.

Success for Sarah no longer meant being busy or constantly climbing higher. It became about balance, purpose, and health. By focusing on what mattered most at work and at home, she achieved more than ever, not in the number of hours she worked, but in the quality of her life. She was successful, without the burnout that once haunted her.

I'm sure many of you can relate to Sarah's story—I know I do. Early in my own career, I thought I could do it all. At one point, I held a full-time position as an Associate Professor of Geriatrics and a part-time role as a minister, all while managing my family life. I had energy and felt I could succeed in both roles. And for a while, I did. I love the following quote and wish I had found it a long time ago:

"Just because you <u>can</u> do it all,

Doesn't mean you <u>should</u>."

(anon.)

But over time, my passion waned, and I became exhausted. I realized something had to give. Within a few months, I stepped back from both jobs and took time to discern the next chapter of my journey. I learned to set new goals and pace myself.

My passion is helping people, so I embarked on certifications in coaching, conflict reconciliation, and healing arts, but I allowed space for rest and time with family and friends. I started my own business, ARISE Leadership Consulting, focusing on helping professional women over 45 enhance their leadership abilities and find success without burnout.

Achieving success without burning out is crucial for women over 45, many of whom are balancing career, personal life, and health.

Here's a roadmap—supported by statistics—on how women can thrive without sacrificing their well-being:

As you reach 45 and beyond, your idea of success may shift.

According to a study by AARP, 51% of women in this age group now value flexibility over pay when considering job opportunities. Success may no longer be defined by promotions or financial gain, but by balance, fulfillment, and personal growth. Instead of focusing on working more hours, think about where you can have the most significant impact. The *Journal of Occupational Health Psychology* found that women who prioritize meaningful work are more satisfied and less likely to experience burnout. It's time to shift focus to what truly matters in your life.

By your 40s and 50s, you have decades of experience and knowledge under your belt.

Research shows that women over 45 are 70% more likely to mentor others compared to their younger counterparts. This allows you to pass on your wisdom and contribute to the growth of others, without constantly chasing higher titles. Additionally, your experience puts you in a strong position to negotiate for flexibility. According to the *Society for Human Resource Management (SHRM)*, nearly 80% of women over 45 value flexible work arrangements, which are essential for maintaining long-term career satisfaction.

As women age, energy levels naturally fluctuate, especially due to hormonal changes like menopause.

Physical well-being is critical—research from the *National Institutes of Health* suggests that regular exercise can reduce fatigue by up to 20%. Keeping your body active helps maintain energy and combats burnout. Mental health is just as important. A study from the *Mental Health Foundation* found that 68% of women over 45 who practiced mindfulness or saw a therapist experienced reduced stress and improved productivity. Additionally, setting clear boundaries in both your personal and professional life is essential—research from *Harvard Business Review* shows women who set firm boundaries are 30% less likely to experience burnout.

A strong support network is crucial to long-term success.

Women who have supportive mentors or peers are 75% more likely to thrive in leadership roles, according to *Forbes*. Surrounding yourself with like-minded individuals helps create a community of encouragement and shared wisdom. Delegating tasks is also a critical skill for reducing stress. Studies from *Stanford University* show that women who delegate reduce their stress levels by up to 33%, giving them more time to focus on high-priority work while maintaining balance.

Staying adaptable is key to thriving in an ever-changing workplace.

According to *Pew Research*, 65% of women over 45 continue learning new skills, allowing them to stay competitive without overwhelming themselves with too much at once. It's also important to pursue personal interests outside of work. Studies show that engaging in hobbies can reduce stress by 30%. Whether it's painting, gardening, or learning a new language, having non-work activities is crucial to recharging your energy and creativity.

At this stage of life, it's often more fulfilling to align your work with your values rather than pursuing constant hustle.

According to a Gallup poll, 60% of women over 45 report greater job satisfaction when their work reflects their personal beliefs and purpose. Giving back through volunteering can also provide a sense of purpose. Research from *Carnegie Mellon* shows that adults who regularly volunteer experience 27% lower stress levels. Finding purpose in service to others can lead to both personal and professional satisfaction.

Achieving financial independence is crucial for long-term success and peace of mind.

Research, like that done by Fidelity Investments, demonstrates that 60% of women over 45 are actively saving for retirement. Building a solid financial foundation can help alleviate stress and provide freedom for future career transitions. Having a clear exit strategy can also ease the pressure of long-term career planning. Studies show that women who plan their transition out of high-pressure roles report 50% less stress and greater satisfaction as they prepare for their next chapter.

It's easy to get caught up in the grind, but reflecting on your achievements is critical.

A *University of California* study found that women who regularly reflect on their accomplishments experience a 40% increase in overall happiness. Taking time to celebrate your growth—both professionally and personally—can bring a sense of fulfillment. Practicing gratitude is another powerful tool for maintaining well-being. By appreciating the positives in your life, you can maintain a balanced and optimistic outlook, even during challenging times.

These strategies, supported by solid research, demonstrate how women over 45 can redefine success, focus on what truly matters, and avoid burnout. This stage of life offers an opportunity to achieve sustainable success without constant striving—where fulfillment, balance, and joy become the new markers of achievement.

As I age, I realize that life is too short to spend it doing something I am not passionate about. Of course, no career is free from the mundane, but my overall purpose is to work in areas where I have passion, the skills to make it work, and the opportunities to learn new and exciting things.

The sooner you begin to protect yourself from burnout the sooner you will find yourself happy content, and even more productive.

"As important as it is to have a plan for doing work,

It is perhaps more important to have

A plan for rest,

Relaxation, self-care

and sleep"

- Akiroq Brost

CALL TO ACTION

A fabulous one-time offer: a free consultation/strategy call with Dr. Suggs, valued at $300: https://form.jotform.com/pksuggs/career-boosting-coaching-call

About The Author

Dr. Patricia Suggs, CEO of ARISE Leadership Consulting, LLC, International Speaker, International Best-Selling Author, ICF Certified Coach, and Expert in Conflict Reconciliation. Throughout her career, she has learned to navigate the biases and discrimination women face (her work began in the late '70s). Her passion is making sure every woman she works with has the knowledge to navigate these waters effectively.

Her work with women 45+ includes strengthening unapologetic self-confidence; learning the techniques to deal with conflict effectively and with compassion; and setting effective boundaries. In addition, Dr. Suggs helps women become more observant in the workplace, understand the politics, become more visible, and find their voice. The key attributes of a great leader to Dr. Suggs are authenticity, integrity, and compassion.

Her goals are to inspire and coach high-achieving professionals both corporately and individually to step out of their comfort zone and become the valued, authentic, and unapologetic leaders they wish to be as they help their teams and businesses succeed and grow. Whether you work in corporate, or small businesses, or are an entrepreneur, Dr. Suggs will help you strategize, meet your goals, and protect you from burnout.

Education: Ph.D., ME.D., University of North Carolina, Greensboro; M.Div., Duke University School of Divinity.
Certifications: ICF for Coaching; Conflict Resolution; Healing Touch.
Work History: Minister; and Associate Professor in Geriatrics at Wake Forest University School of Medicine; and presently Speaker, Writer, Coach/Consultant

Contact Info

ARISE Leadership Consulting, LLC
www.ariseleadershipconsulting.com
patricia@pksuggscoaching.net
https://www.linkedin.com/in/drpatriciasuggs

"To my deceased husband Robert, whose patience and joy were the support I needed to find, live and share my authenticity."

THE AUTHENTIC PATH: ACHIEVING SUCCESS WITHOUT SACRIFICING YOURSELF

by Dr. Norma Hollis

Chapter 16

The Authentic Path: Achieving Success Without Sacrificing Yourself

by Dr. Norma Hollis

It was a revelation for me to learn that the number one regret of seniors in nursing homes is living a life that wasn't true to themselves. They spent their lives chasing someone else's idea of success, sacrificing their authenticity in the process. In the busyness of life, they didn't honor their dreams and as their life was concluding, they realized that their choices led to unfulfilled dreams.

This realization is heartbreaking, considering that each of us is born with unique gifts and talents. Yet, as we navigate life, we are often steered away from our authentic paths, sometimes gently, sometimes forcefully.

My life became frustrating at age 28 when I recognized that the person I was becoming was the person my parents thought best but was unrecognizable to me.

That started my journey of studying human nature for over 30 years to come up with programs that help people find, live and share their authenticity. Using my education and experience, I've dedicated my life to transforming people's lives by helping them find their authentic self, live their authentic life, and share their authentic voice.

I wrote this chapter to provide essential tips to help you find, live and share your authenticity first with yourself, and if desired, with the world.

Finding Your Authentic Self

At some point in life, we were all completely authentic. For most of us, that time was during infancy, before societal norms influenced us. Imagine singing your heart out in preschool, only to be discouraged by family members who didn't cheer you on. This is often the beginning of the many layers of masks we wear to conform to expectations set by others— family, teachers, friends, lovers, and bosses all have their say

Many people are told to "just be authentic," as if it's something you can achieve overnight. But true authenticity requires an inward journey to reconnect with your passions, reflect on life experiences, acknowledge your expertise, and align the different aspects of yourself. Each of us is complex, with multiple dimensions that we often lose sight of. To be authentic, you need to reconnect with your passions, reflect on your experiences, and align your energy with your strengths.

Finding your authentic self is the first step to living authentically and its foundation is within your inner voice. This is the private voice that whispers quietly inside of you. Everyone has this voice but sometimes people do not recognize it. It's the voice that answers the question when you ask what time it is, what shall I wear today or what am I going to eat? It's also the voice that speaks to us when we should or shouldn't do something, call someone, turn right rather than left and so many other messages that come daily. The problem we have is accurately listening to, trusting and following that voice. The key to finding your authentic self is developing the ability to listen to and trust the authentic voice that speaks within you.

"Many people are told to 'just be authentic'
as if it's something you can achieve overnight."

The second step is to recognize your passions, acknowledge your experiences – good and bad, and recognize your expertise, often based on multiple years practicing the same profession.

Your authenticity is linked to your inner energy. When you understand and align this energy with your passion, experiences, and expertise, you gain a deeper understanding of what makes you unique. I developed an assessment to help you identify your authenticity strengths and vulnerabilities. Start this process by taking the <u>Authenticity Assessment</u>, which will guide you to reflect on your authenticity in new ways.

Living Your Authentic Life

I recently interviewed several dozen people and discovered two common challenges when it comes to living with authenticity; speaking up and understanding what authenticity truly feels like. Many fear expressing their true thoughts, worried about embarrassment or offending others. This results in suppressing their own needs—saying "yes" when they want to say "no" or keeping quiet to avoid conflict.

The fear of speaking up is common. We don't want to embarrass ourselves or others so we often say what we think people want to hear, like agreeing with your boss even when you know your perspective is valuable or staying silent in a relationship to avoid conflict. Have you ever stayed silent to avoid hurting someone's feelings but ended up hurting yourself instead? To live truly authentic, you must speak up, even if it's uncomfortable or risky. Just do it with respect for the situation. The reward? Joy. When I found my authentic life, I moved from feelings of anxiety to joy and fulfillment.

At eight, I developed a hole in my eardrum that caused severe pain for two years. For decades, I viewed this time as traumatic. One day, I realized I could change my perspective. Instead of seeing my life as a story of pain, I reframed it as a story of triumph. The pain in my ear caused me to pause and listen more closely to the inner voice that spoke within me. This shift not only changed how I viewed my past but also how I live and work today.

I activated my authenticity and transformed myself from a sad and melancholy view of life to a view that not only felt joyful, but inspired others to be joyful as well. Living your authentic life is about finding your joy and embracing it. Some people think that more money results in more joy, but this is a false belief. Joy is not related to money but to peace of mind. It is one of the most profound benefits of authenticity.

How are you living your authenticity? Do you love what you do? Do you speak up and let others know what's on your mind? Are you on the edge of burnout? Do you prefer to live with joy rather than burnout? You are invited to join me every second Tuesday at 5:00 PM Pacific for a complimentary group dialogue where I help people activate and live with authenticity. Discover how others live authentically and gain insights into your own journey.

Sharing Your Authentic Voice

One of our most fundamental desires as humans is to self-actualize—to live creatively, purposefully, and meaningfully. This is our nature as children, full of optimism about what we can achieve. Yet, as we grow older, the realities of life often stifle our creativity. Income-generating activities take precedence, and our creative aspirations often fade.

Expressing your authenticity is crucial for personal fulfillment. According to Maslow's hierarchy of needs, our basic physiological needs must be met before we can focus on higher pursuits like self-actualization. However, younger generations, such as Millennials and Gen Z, often reverse this order. They prioritize self-actualization over traditional measures of success. This shift challenges conventional norms but is essential for expressing one's true self.

"Expressing your authenticity is crucial for personal fulfillment."

Many of us over 50 are considering how to transition from our current roles to something that truly fulfills us. This shift can be daunting, requiring us to let go of the familiar and embrace the unknown. But if we don't make this change, we risk living with the regret of not following our hearts.

Sharing your authentic voice is not just related to speaking, although it is excellent advice for those in the speaking industry. Authentic voice also has a broader meaning when you consider that your authentic voice is the same as your purpose. The natural gifts and talents you were given, combined with your passion, experience and expertise, lead you to identify your purpose and inspire you to embrace it. One of the greatest benefits of being authentic is that you become a phenomenal role model for the generations coming behind you.

"Imagine a world where authenticity is the norm and regrets about not being authentic do not exist. It's possible and it starts with you."

If this resonates with you, it's time to determine how you want to express yourself in the decades ahead. Don't let fear or societal expectations hold you back from living your truth. If you are serious and want direction to transform your life, schedule a <u>private complimentary call</u> with me. **Wishing you a phenomenal life of finding, living and sharing your authenticity in joyful ways!**

CALL TO ACTION

Isn't it time you give joy a try? Take Norma's Authenticity Assessment and learn more about how you are showing up as authentic you. http://www.AuthenticityAssessment.com.

About The Author

Norma Hollis, Hon. Ph.D. is a transformational strategist who writes, develops and implements programs for human development. She is a professional speaker and phenomenal coach specializing in transforming the lives of women who want to live the authentic life they were born for. She has been deemed one of the top 100 coaches by Coaching.com, an international organization where she serves as a coach host for ongoing training. She is a leading authority on authenticity and is affectionately known as the Godmother of Authenticity. Her programs and services are grounded in her Authenticity Grid, the result of 30 years of research into human nature.

Dr. Hollis has been a pioneer in three industries – early childhood, professional speaking and coaching. She blended her knowledge in these three areas and created the Authenticity Grid, a graphic representation of her 30-year journey into human nature. People across the globe use her Grid as a self-coaching tool to help them to find their authentic self, live their authentic life, and share their authentic voice.

Dr. Hollis is the author of many books, programs and online classes to help people get on their authentic path. She offers multiple online classes and certified coaches who lead you in group or individual settings to activate your authenticity and live a
life of unspeakable joy.

Contact Info

Authenticity U
http://www.NormaHollis.com
info@normahollis.com
https://www.linkedin.com/in/normahollis/

"Burnout is not a badge of honour."
Arianna Huffington

"With special gratitude to my husband, Steve, for always believing in me."

THE LIFE COACH'S PATH TO EXCITING SUCCESS WITHOUT BURNOUT

by Wendy Vaughan

Chapter 17

The Life Coach's Path to Exciting Success Without Burnout

By Wendy Vaughan, Business Success Coach

The Balancing Act of Transformation

As heart-centered coaches, we have a special calling to help others work through their personal barriers and turn frustrations and fears into exciting realities. Making an impact is deeply fulfilling work, but it also comes with its own challenges. When you're so focused on giving and making a difference for others, you risk overextending yourself and undercharging, which leads to exhaustion, frustration, and even burnout.

In this chapter, I'll share how you can continue to serve with passion and compassion and build a thriving Six Figure business that nourishes both you and your clients. You'll discover how to honor your vision of making a big impact without sacrificing your personal well-being.

The Invisible Cost of Overgiving

Let's start by addressing the trap many heart-centred coaches unknowingly fall into over-giving. You love supporting and empowering others, so you give and give – your time, your energy, and your heart. It feels honourable to serve, but when you give without boundaries, it comes at a cost.

During my first 5 years as a coach, I undercharged for my services. I thought my clients were struggling financially so even though I helped them gain the skills to get clients, I didn't want to cause them financial stress - at least that was my thinking at the time (more about that later!).

I constantly over-delivered. As an empath and highly intuitive coach, I poured myself into my clients before, during, and after every coaching session. One Friday evening, after finishing up on a client's marketing copy, I calculated how much time I was investing in each client. And based on my rates I realized I was working for minimum wage! And the worst part? I spent all my extra time working on getting my next client. Eventually, my passion was replaced with exhaustion. Can you relate?

This is so common among heart-centered coaches. It's so easy to give and give because it feels so rewarding. But the truth is, when you over-give, you're depleting yourself, and you're also diminishing the patience, compassion, and creativity needed to fully support your clients to navigate all their self-sabotaging patterns!

Charging More Without Guilt

One of the most difficult things for heart-centered professionals is to own their value and charge what they're truly worth. Even though you're dedicated to helping people discover their highest truth, we often accept their stories about their struggles and scarcity, and that makes us hesitate when it comes to charging more or raising our rates.

And as I mentioned earlier, when you feel guilty about charging your clients and worry about your rates being too high for them, it means you're focused on money stories.

But here's the truth: the cost of anything is relative. And when you attach your rates to the real-life transformation you provide - including the ripple effects, your potential clients become excited about investing in themselves.

And, when you don't charge enough, your clients may not value the transformation you're offering them - and typically they don't invest as much of their time or energy in taking the actions you're recommending.

By showcasing the real-life transformation your work provides, you're not only empowering yourself but also empowering your clients with belief and excitement!

The Cost of Burnout

Burnout is the silent enemy of success. Many heart-centered coaches who are finally able to attract a steady flow of clients find themselves trapped in a vicious cycle—working long hours, posting on social media ad nauseum, building out new marketing funnels, undercharging for their services and then taking on too many clients in an attempt to make a decent living. And instead of feeling fueled by the profound impact they're making, they find themselves feeling burned out. Is that really *success*?

"Burnout is the silent enemy of success."

As you know, burnout is physical, mental, and emotional depletion. It's a loss of creativity, and a disconnection from your original excitement and passion. All motivation stalls out - especially self-care. And have you ever been married to someone who's burned out? Eesh! And then the cycle completes itself because now that passion to empower others has turned into resentment. When you're burned out, you can't show up fully for your clients, which eventually leads to no clients because it's all become a grind.

So, how do you have a thriving business without sacrificing yourself?

Strategies for Sustainable Success

Here's the good news: it's entirely possible to build and run a successful Six-Figure business without burning out. The key is to work smarter, not harder. Here are some proven strategies that have worked for heart-centered coaches like you:

1. Prioritize Self-Care

Your well-being is essential to your success. If you're not taking care of yourself, you can't take care of your clients. Make self-care a non-negotiable part of your daily routine. This includes setting boundaries, scheduling regular breaks, and making time for activities that replenish your mind, body, and spirit.

2. Leverage Your Time and Energy

Time management is crucial to avoiding burnout. Focus on high-impact actions that generate business-building results, not just random activity. Techniques like time-blocking and the Pomodoro method can help you manage your time more effectively. And what's most important is being intentional about what happens during that time block!

3. Automate and Delegate

Delegation and automation are not signs of weakness—they're signs of wisdom. Automate routine tasks like client onboarding, social media posting, and email marketing. Hire virtual assistants to handle administrative work and utilize software systems and AI to streamline your operations. This way you can focus on what you do best: serving your clients.

4. Maximize Impact with Minimal Effort

Create a signature, high-impact program that allows you to serve multiple high-end clients at once without overextending yourself. High Impact, High-Value Group Coaching Programs enable you to serve more people without increasing your workload. Focus on marketing strategies that leverage your time ***and get results*** - meaning clients! Work smart vs hard.

5. Stay Connected to Your Passion

Burnout often happens when we lose touch with the original passion that led us to this work. Regularly revisit your "why." Put visual reminders in your workspace. Stay connected with like-minded peers, join mastermind groups, and create new initiatives that reignite your excitement for your work. Passion is the fuel that keeps you going - nourish and protect it!

Scaling to Six Figures Without Burnout

Building a Six-Figure business doesn't have to mean working more hours or sacrificing your wellness and personal life. In fact, the most successful heart-centered coaches have learned how to scale their businesses while working fewer hours. Here's how:

- **Attract Ideal Clients:** By focusing on attracting ideal clients who are craving the outcomes your work delivers, and they're ready and willing to invest in their transformation, you can step out of the lower-end trap.

- **Charge What You're Worth:** When you raise your rates to reflect the true value of the transformation you provide, you step into a deeper level of impact, while making more income. This allows you to create a sustainable business that doesn't rely on constant client churn.

- **Create Scalable Offers:** Group programs, workshops, and other scalable offers allow you to attract and serve more clients without taking more of your time so you can increase your impact and your income.

"It's all about creating a deeply fulfilling business that supports your well-being and allows you to live the life you truly desire."

Achieve Exciting Success Without Sacrificing Yourself

The path to having a business that fuels your passion, and your lifestyle is not about giving endlessly until you have nothing left. It's about balancing your desire to serve with a commitment to your own well-being while working smart. By redefining your worth, setting boundaries, and leveraging your time and energy, you can build a thriving Six Figure business that allows you to make a bigger impact without burning out - and your friends and family will enjoy you more, too!

Make it a Reality! Get the Passion to Six Figures Business Blueprint

If you're ready to take the next step and learn exactly how to build a scalable, passion-driven business that's generating Six Figures while requiring about 20 hours per week to run, I invite you to download the free **Passion to Six Figures Business Blueprint for Heart-Centered Coaches**. This blueprint will guide you step-by-step through the exact process to create a thriving business without sacrificing your well-being.

CALL TO ACTION

Click <u>HERE</u> to download your free Passion to Six Figures Blueprint!

If you're ready to take the next step and learn exactly how to build a scalable, passion-driven business that's generating Six Figures while requiring about 20 hours per week to run, I invite you to download the free Passion to Six Figures Business Blueprint for Heart-Centered Coaches. This blueprint will guide you step-by-step through the exact process to create a thriving business without sacrificing your well-being. Click HERE to download your free Blueprint!

https://passiontosixfigures.com/six-figure-business-blueprint

About The Author

Wendy Vaughan is a Business Success Coach with 28 years of business development experience. She's passionate about helping heart-centered coaches build thriving, Six Figure businesses that align with their passion and purpose.

As an empath and a recovering perfectionist, Wendy knows firsthand that the biggest barrier to success is often ourselves. With a blend of intuition, compassion, and strategy, she empowers her clients to own their value and stop playing small.

Heart-centered life coaches hire Wendy to help them build a thriving, passion-driven business because they're sick and tired of playing small, posting content on social media ad nauseum, and being frustrated by complicated marketing funnels that don't work.

So, she empowers them to create a fulfilling High Ticket Program, attract and enroll clients with ease, and make a profound impact.Bottom line, Wendy helps coaches add Six Figures in sales in two years or less, guaranteed.

Wendy currently lives in Hawaii, actively living her dream alongside her devoted husband of 29 years. She is also an avid outrigger canoe paddler and enjoys captaining their 22-foot power catamaran exploring the beautiful coral reefs of Moloka'i.

Wendy firmly believes that if you've been prompted to make a meaningful difference for others, there's no reason you cannot have a thriving business that makes a profound impact and creates a beautiful lifestyle for yourself.

Contact Info

Predictable Sales Results Inc: The Passion to Six Figures Initiative
https://predictablesalesresults.com/
Wendy@PredictableSalesResults.com
https://www.linkedin.com/in/wendy-vaughan-business-coach/

"Real change, enduring change, happens one step at a time."
Ruth Bader Ginsburg

"To my family"

SYNERGY AND OUTSOURCING

by Brian Crew

Chapter 18

The Secret to Success Without Burning Out: Selecting Synergy and Outsource to Partners

Brian Crew

Success is how we define it. So, to burnout in the process of becoming successful would in most cases mean you weren't successful. I don't think anyone attempts to become burnt out on their road or journey to success and true success is a journey not a destination.

By definition, the key to becoming successful would be your ability to manage those elements that will stress you out and create burnout. There are two paths to avoid burnout. The first path would be to balance all your priorities and responsibilities to achieve success. The second path would be to focus on what you're good at and what is key to your business and get others to do those other priorities or tasks that need to be done.

Choosing synergy makes cents and dollars

One of the keys choices you'll end up having to make is around what will be in scope and out of scope in terms of the work you're doing.

It's very challenging when a customer or client or potential client asks you to do something that you're quite capable of achieving yet this is not part of your regular service offering, it's very tempting to say yes. But choosing synergy over pleasing your client will reduce your burnout, stress, reduce your time pressures, and increase your satisfaction by doing a better job and not stretching yourself too thin just to please a client and collect additional money. By choosing synergy, your service offerings are repeatable for each client, each time, each month so that you're not creating new solutions each time and you have a series of solutions would you continue to apply to each client repeatedly and not expanding that scope and staying within those parameters is synergy.

By ensuring your service offerings are synergistic this makes your offerings easier to understand to prospects and increases your profitability by reducing your cost on service development. This also increases your reputation in your field and increases your probability within your operation.

Operational Synergy includes outsourcing

On the operations and back-office side of your business it's also working to stay synergistic. In small organizations most roles tend to have a wide scope of duties and responsibilities compared to larger organizations where roles are much more focused. In order to maintain the focus necessary on the operational side and back-office side, it's key to limit the functions and responsibilities of roles. So those functions and responsibilities that don't easily fit into a role or aren't aligned with the strength of your employees or yourself, should be the functions considered to be outsourced. Any activity that is not core to your generating profits should be outsourced whether it's back office or operations.

Everything from bookkeeping, manufacturing, to sales and marketing all should be considered for outsourcing. What's key when outsourcing is ensuring synergy and by that, I mean that the functions that are outsourced are easily plug and play and fit into the process inside the organization. For example, you can outsource your marketing and prospecting and have highly qualified leads generated for you to hand off to the salesperson who does the pitching, closing, and negotiating of contracts. The skill set for marketing and prospecting is very different from that of being a closer in the sales function does it makes logical sense to outsource sales and prospecting and keeping the closing which is critical to your revenue quality

The age-old methodology of keeping everything that is critical inside your organization no longer works in today's world. Hiring fractional expertise and outsourcing is a more effective message to compete with larger competitors.

Remember synergy

What's critical in the success of this model is to maintain synergy. On the revenue side stay focused on offering only synergistic services and on the back office in operation side it's key to ensure you maintain synergy among all your functions and processes. The return on investment you can expect by outsourcing is significant. Organizations who outsource their prospecting ensuring synergy with the rest of the sales process can easily see 50 to 85% savings in the cost of the operations. The other key benefit of outsourcing is the time savings, which can be equally significant.

"Organizations who outsource their prospecting ensuring synergy with the rest of the sales process can easily see 50 to 85% savings in the cost of the operations."

CALL TO ACTION

Book a complimentary call with Brian: https://calendly.com/briancrew/30

About The Author

Brian is a creative solution architect, people developer, strategic thinker and data-oriented planner. With a true passion for creating and growing businesses from idea to completion.

Brian is an energetic and creative executive with experience in leading businesses to growth and profits. He has consistently led various businesses to outperform expectations and create, develop and deliver strategic and business plans.

He has 25 plus years of business experience that has honed his business acumen and perfected his team leadership skills.

Brian has 10 years' experience with Ernst & Young Corporate Consulting focused on change management, performance improvement, data analysis and performance measurement.

Brian also has 13 years in senior leadership positions in various small businesses in various industries from "Bay Street" to food services. Brian has turned around various businesses improving profitability, building teams, and establishing strategies. Brian has the rare ability to see the big picture which allows him to formulate creative solutions.

Brian has created and developed a proprietary Sales Prospecting Model that is LinkedIn based. The model helps B2B Service providers double revenues and reduce costs.

Brian is also involved with his local community in Richmond Hill where he lives with his wife and 2 children for over a decade.

Contact Info
BricConsulting
brian@bricconsulting.ca
https://www.linkedin.com/in/briancrew

Conclusion

Success Without Burnout – Your New Way Forward

You've made it to the end, but this isn't just the conclusion—it's your starting point. This book wasn't just about showing you how to win big; it was about doing it **without losing yourself** along the way. Success and well-being are no longer opposing forces—they are partners in your journey.

In our fast-paced world, burnout has become the unfortunate side effect of ambition. But you now know that it doesn't have to be this way. When you prioritize **self-awareness, meaningful connections, and balance**, you set yourself up for sustainable success. Living fully in the present while building a future you love means aligning your actions with your values—both at work and in life.

There will always be challenges, but armed with the insights from these pages, you'll have the tools to navigate them with confidence and resilience. You'll know how to **set boundaries**, **lead with impact**, and **create space for rest** without guilt. Success, after all, isn't just about how far you go—it's about how well you live along the way.

Now it's your turn to apply what you've learned. **Reflect, reset, and take action.** Be the leader, creator, and change-maker you were born to be—without compromising your well-being. **Your success story starts now—and this time, it's one you'll enjoy every step of the way.**

Thank you for taking this journey with us. Here's to winning big, living well, and making a lasting impact—without burnout. Let's redefine success, together.

Powerful Women Today
Championing and Empowering Emotional and Financial Independence
www.powerfulwomentoday.com

Acknowledgments

This book is a result of collaboration, inspiration, and shared passion. To every PWT Mentor Expert colleague and friend who believed in the vision of success without burnout—thank you.

Your insights and encouragement made this journey possible. To our readers, thank you for trusting us with your time and energy. You are the reason this message matters, and we are honoured to walk this path with you. Let's continue building lives filled with purpose, balance, and joy.

CALL TO ACTION

Ready to take your growth to the next level?

Join the **PWT Global Network**, Success Without Burnout Virtual Mastermind where leaders and changemakers connect to share resources, strategies, and inspiration.

Surround yourself with a community that uplifts, supports, and encourages sustainable success. It's time to grow together—join us today!

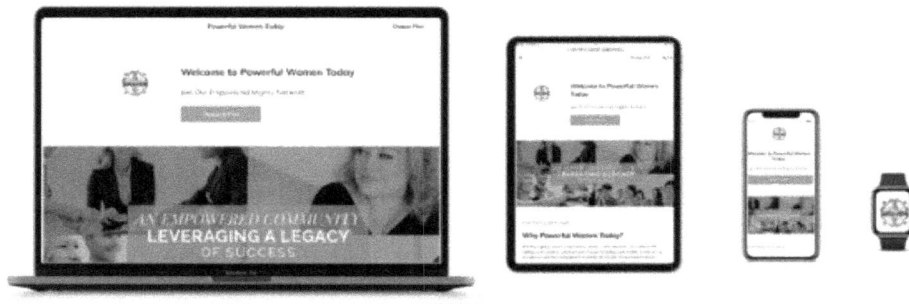

Empowered Global Network
Championing Women & Allies
Connecting Success